THE GAME
WITHIN
THE GAME

THE GAME
WITHIN
THE GAME

Walt Frazier

WITH DAN MARKOWITZ

NEW YORK

ISBN: 1-4013-0253-X

Hyperion books are available for special promotions and premiums. For details contact Michael Rentas, Assistant Director, Inventory Operations, Hyperion, 77 West 66th Street, 11th floor, New York, New York 10023–6201, or call 212-456-0133.

FIRST EDITION

10 9 8 7 6 5 4 3 2 1

To my loving parents and Uncle Chill for providing the impetus; to my former coaches, teammates, and opponents for their invigorating challenge and fortitude; and to my friends and fans for their love, respect, and support.

—W.F.

To Jeanne, for all her love and support. To my new son, Callum, who inspires me. To my mother, Selma, and father, Joe, who encouraged my love of basketball and writing. Finally, to Walt "Clyde" Frazier, for collaborating on this book in which he shared so many wonderful stories with me about a game we both love.

—D.M.

ACKNOWLEDGMENTS

I'd like to thank Bob Miller and Gretchen Young of Hyperion for giving Dan Markowitz and myself the opportunity to write this book. I'd like to thank Bill Bradley, who played a pretty mean "game within the game," for writing the Foreword to this book.

—Walt Frazier

I'd like to thank Bob Miller and Gretchen Young of Hyperion for making this book happen. Bob came up with the title and Gretchen was as positive and as thorough an editor as I could have imagined. Her vision, kindness, and calm head and hand were the main reasons this book reached its conclusion. I cannot thank Gretchen enough for the work she has done.

Ruth Curry, Gretchen's assistant, was a reliable and friendly voice on the other end of the phone, in helping put this book together. Joshua Cohen, the copy editor, did a wonderful job in parsing the grammar and syntax in the writing, and adding his hoops insight. Andrew Gottlieb did a remarkable job updating the book. My agent, Lisa Queen, and her assistant, Jessica Gribetz, were there to put out the many fires that were ignited in the writing and publishing. I'd like to thank them both for the instrumental roles that they played.

Special thanks to Senator Bill Bradley, Kenny Smith of Turner Sports, Jack McCallum of *Sports Illustrated*, Ric Bucher of ESPN, Phil Chenier, and John Starks. I enjoyed talking the game of basketball with all of you and hearing your insights on the game within the game and Clyde.

In no particular order, many thanks also go to Marty Burns of *Sports Illustrated*; Tim Frank, Mark Broussard, Rob Reheuser, John Gardella, Helen Wong, and Lori Kashouty of the National Basketball Association; Joe Favorito, Jonathan Supranowitz, Sammy Steinlight, and Dennis D'Agostino of the New York Knicks; Zack Bolno of the Washington Wizards; Steve Bulpett of the *Boston Herald*; Jeff Pomeroy of Turner Sports; and basketball expert Chris Ekstrand. Without your cordial help I never could have assembled the statistics and facts for this book. I appreciate your professionalism and the time you gave me.

Last but not least, I'd like to thank my wife, Jeanne, who transcribed hours and hours of tape. Her interest in and knowledge of basketball and her eyes for good writing proved to be invaluable.

—Dan Markowitz

CONTENTS

Contents

FOREWORD

by Senator Bill Bradley

The game within the game is the game that only the players see. They experience it in relation to one another on the floor at a particular time and in the middle of the action. It is one of the nuances of the game of basketball.

As Knick teammates during those years, we knew what a teammate was going to do almost before he did it. We helped one another on defense and shared the ball on offense. We made room for each of us to be his best within the context of the team. For example, I often would see Clyde come down the floor with the ball. I'd catch his eye. I knew he wanted to go down my side of the floor. In order to give him a little more room to move, I would clear out. That way I didn't clog up his space. Or, when I had the ball on the side and he was at the top of the key, waiting to go backdoor, our center knew he had to move to the other side of the floor to create the room for the backdoor bounce pass from me to

Clyde who was moving down the lane toward the basket. That was the game within the game. On one level, the game within the game was a matter of mechanics but it also operated on a psychological level in that we truly were all for one and one for all. We challenged one another in practice to become better. We helped one another come back from defeat. We inspired one another to reach our peak team performance. None of us felt we could be as good alone as all of us could be together. Our unity came sometimes with laughs, sometimes with conflicts, sometimes with moments of collective insight, but it was that spirit of camaraderie which brought us together in a way that allowed the fans to see something very special. In retrospect, we were lucky to have the chance to play before the roar of 19,500 spectators, and feel the chills go up and down our spines, and hear the crowd applaud rebounds and the pass that led to the pass that led to the basket—not simply the score. Much of that Madison Square Garden audience, it seemed, understood the game within the game too.

Since 1977, not counting the five jersey retirements of my teammates at Madison Square Garden, I have attended probably fewer than 20 games. I don't usually watch regular-season games but I try never to miss the fifth and seventh games of the Eastern Conference playoffs, the Western Conference playoffs, and the finals. I watch on TV when the money is on the line.

To me the game has changed in a number of ways: When we played, the game was played with your feet and it was about finesse. Now the game is played with your upper body and it's about strength. Second, they don't call fouls closely enough now. Therefore, again, it's an upper-body game, more like sumo wrestling than it is ballet. When we played, I thought it was ballet, and if there ever was a Baryshnikov of basketball, it was Clyde.

The three-point rule also has changed the game. When we played, the objective was to get the easiest shot closest to the basket and you did that by team movement. Now, you have a pick-and-roll on one side and six guys standing at 30 feet on the other, and the ball being thrown all the way across court when the pick-and-roll fails. Players can hit the three-point shot, but there are not a whole lot of guys who can shoot the 18-foot jump shot off the dribble while being guarded. The ball rarely goes in to a center and then out to a forward and then back in to the center. There are only occasional backdoor plays. It's a more stagnant game. It's not that interesting for me to watch.

The team bond on the Knicks came from many different things but certainly one of them was our shared experience of the road. We traveled together. We were in airports together, on planes together. Each of us had to make the bus in the morning to the airport or from the hotel to a road game. After games we often went our separate ways but in a very fundamental sense we lived together on the road. That bred a familiarity that contributed to unity. Today you get the impression that guys often share less of their time with teammates and more with an entourage.

I am also unhappy to see the influx of high school players in the league today. Not that some young players are not having successful careers, but from a maturity standpoint I think there's a value in having the college experience and I think the NBA's decision to establish an age requirement of 19 for draft eligibility is a step in the right direction. Players often say, "Well, if we make four million dollars a year, we have to take the money. Then we can always go back to school." When you're making four million a year, you might say you'll go back to school in order to get a long-term job that pays a hundred thousand a year, but many players don't return to school and get that degree. They often don't see the joy education can bring throughout a lifetime. They get carried away by the salary numbers and the lifestyle, which is their right, but it's a shame on a human level.

Once you win a championship you share a special rapport with your teammates. It is one of those things that just is. For example, when Clyde called me to write this foreword, I said, "Sure, no problem." My teammates replied the same way to me when I asked them to campaign for me in politics. When you go to the mountaintop together, you are brothers for life. The bond is permanent because of what we gave to one another and what we achieved. Winning the NBA title is an experience that very few people know. We were lucky enough to share it twice, and part of our success came from our collective ability to play the game within the game.

THE GAME
WITHIN
THE GAME

INTRODUCTION

In my first pre-season game, back in 1967, I had to guard Hal Greer. He was one of my heroes, probably my favorite NBA player, and I was excited to test myself against the best. But that night he just killed me. He beat me off the dribble, he pulled up for 15-foot jumpers. He actually made me foul out. Hal Greer humiliated me so badly that after the game, when the locker room cleared out, I sat down and cried. I thanked God that I had signed a three-year contract because I really didn't think I had what it took to make it in the NBA.

Less than three years later, I had the best game of my career scoring 36 points, dishing out 19 assists, grabbing 7 rebounds, and recording 4 steals against the Lakers in Game 7 of the 1970 NBA Finals. We won the championship that day and I joined Jerry West and Oscar Robertson as one of the top guards in the game. I was a star. I wound up in the Hall of Fame and I was even awarded the highest honor that a basketball player can receive: I was named one of the 50 greatest players of all time.

What happened in between Hal Greer sending me into the doldrums and my becoming a member of the basketball elite? How did I bridge the gap from depression to elation? Well, I worked hard at improving all aspects of my game. I got stronger mentally and physically. I had good coaching, I studied the other players, and I learned from the history of the NBA. I gained confidence, ability, and intelligence. In short: I learned the game within the game.

Today's players are unlike anything the game has ever seen before. You've got Dirk Nowitzki, a 7-footer with infinite range. There's LeBron James, who is as strong as Willis Reed and as quick as Bob Cousy. And you've got Kobe Bryant, who can jump out of the gym and score from anywhere on the court. But are today's teams better than any teams in the history of the game? No—but they could be. Are today's players getting as much out of their games as the great players have before? I don't think so— but, if they did, you'd see a new breed of superstar.

Basketball is the greatest game ever. And NBA basketball is the greatest of the great. When I watch an NBA game, I feel like I'm seeing the best athletes in the world. I saw a lot as a player. As an announcer, I've watched countless games from the best seat in the house. And all along I've been carefully observing our sport. I see where it's better than ever and I see where it needs some help. Over the years I've been a fan, a player, an agent, and a commentator. I owe everything to basketball. This book is a collection of my thoughts about the game. Some are criticisms, some are suggestions, some are anecdotes, and some are just dreams. But together they make up the blueprint to what I call the game within the game.

In these pages, I'm going to tell you exactly what I've seen out on the court over the past 40 years. I'm going to illuminate the game within the game, calling on my experiences having played against elite players like Bill Russell, Jerry West, Kareem Abdul-Jabbar, and Dr. J, and, as a broadcaster, having analyzed Michael Jordan, Tim Duncan, Shaq, Dwyane Wade, and Kobe. If the next wave of stars—LeBron or Steve Nash or Amare Stoudemire—are going to win a championship next season, or in years to come, first they will have to learn to win the game within the game.

 *Chapter 1*

SUBSTANCE OVER STYLE

A few years ago at Madison Square Garden, a father came up to me with his son and asked him, "Do you know who this man is?"

The son smiled and said, "Sure, that's Walt Frazier, the Knicks' announcer."

"No," the father smiled, "this is Walt 'Clyde' Frazier, the player. Before Michael Jordan there was Walt Frazier."

Before Magic Johnson and Larry Bird, Dr. J carried the league. But after Magic and Bird, it was Michael. He was a phenomenal player, probably the best the game has ever seen. Michael and I both brought an artistic flair to the game. We both embellished a certain style. We shared a flair for the dramatic. Like people would say, "When the game's on the line, Clyde's going to do something special." Then I would hit the winning shot and just run off the court like it was halftime.

Jordan was an artist because like my former adversary and then teammate, Earl "the Pearl" Monroe, you never knew what he was going to do. Jordan would go in the air and take your breath away, dunking on guys, making big shots, swooping up on the defense and coming up with steals. There was just an incredible array of things that the guy could do.

But when people talk about Jordan, they mostly talk about his dunks. He was an All-Defensive player, one of the smartest players in the game, but no one ever focuses on that. Players don't want to emulate his defense; they want to dunk like Mike. They celebrate his playground style, and trivialize the old-school basketball substance of his game.

But what made Michael truly great was his innate understanding of the game within the game. Defense wins, hard work pays off, and sometimes the tongue-wagging, tomahawk dunk is meaningless compared to the unheralded first-quarter steal.

Like most NBA players of any generation, my introduction to the game occurred on an outside playground court. But gradually I abandoned the playground for indoor gyms to hone my game. Still, the summer after my rookie season with the Knicks, I returned to the playground to play in the outdoor Harlem Rucker League up on 155th Street in Manhattan. I was on a team with Willis Reed. Chamberlain played on another team, Robertson on another. But I hated it. There were no nets on the rims. It was just showtime. Guys were goaltending, carrying the ball on their dribble. It was just like the game is now in the NBA. It was all about the hoopla.

The fans were out on the court. There was no room with people crowded all the way up to the sidelines and the baselines. They were hanging from fences and up in the trees. It was like a three-ring circus and very intimidating. I'm the Knicks' No. 1 draft choice and I see players jumping all over the place and I've never even heard of them. I'm like, "Wow, man!" It was like when I played for the first time in the old Madison Square Garden and had a bad case of "Gardenitis."

There was a definite allure for the NBA pros to come back and play in the Harlem Rucker League. It allowed us to go back to our roots as players. There is also a definite allure for the modern player to emulate the more spectacular parts of Jordan's game and believe that his ability to make those gravity-defying moves are what made him great. But there are no shortcuts to greatness. Players need to evolve out of their playground game and mentality if they are to become consistent All-Stars and winners in the NBA.

The players up in the Harlem Rucker League would goaltend and the referees would let them get away with it. They all carried the ball on the dribble. They had little discipline to their games. I decided just to buckle down on my defense. I didn't even try to score. I took care of my man and made sure that he wasn't going to score on me. On offense, I just got the ball in to Willis.

It was a pride thing. I was going to shut my man down and not let anyone dunk on me. It's like I was the big gunslinger coming into a new town with my big reputation. *All* the New York City playground legends were trying to show me up. The fans just wanted to see exciting plays and ooh and ah over dunks and blocked shots. They were rooting hard for the local guys, saying, "This guy should be in the NBA." They were pumping up Earl "the Goat" Manigault and Herman "the Helicopter" Knowings, but those guys didn't have it.

Manigault was too short. He really couldn't shoot from the perimeter. He could take you inside, but if he had gotten his chance to play in the NBA he wouldn't have been able to go inside and dunk against Wilt and Russell. He would have had to stay out on the perimeter and shoot the ball from outside. But since New York City playgrounds usually don't have nets on their rims—and the backboards are difficult to bank off—few legendary playground stars shoot well from the outside. They like to penetrate and devastate.

The playground legends were like a lot of the young players in the NBA today. The Goat and the Helicopter didn't mind going 1-for-10 from the field, if that one shot was a big dunk and it brought down the house. Then they went home happy. Just one big dunk to astound and arouse the house and they were happy. Today the NBA game often devolves into a fest of dunks and threes because guys fall into adopting a playground mentality.

I only played in the Rucker League in Harlem that one year. I never went back. I didn't like it. I didn't like playing outside with no nets and all the hoopla. It wasn't about the game and *that's why I wasn't into it*. The game within the game on the playground is seeing who can make the most audacious move and get the biggest fan reaction. It's not about creating a ballet that all five players can dance in, playing with sweet harmony.

ESPN perpetuates the playground dominance of the game with their nightly highlights on *SportsCenter*. The only time you see a stellar defensive play on ESPN is if a player blocks a shot to preserve a win or the highlights embellish Ben Wallace's defensive prowess. Shows like *Street Ball* and games televised on ESPN from the Entertainers Basketball Classic at Rucker Park accentuate the Swiss-cheese defense, clowning, and dunking that have become more prevalent in the NBA game today.

The street ball and playground players are today's version of the Harlem Globetrotters, but they have hurt the development of the game and the integrity of the sport. Kids watch their antics on the court and mimic the way they play. Consequently, they're learning bad fundamentals, showboating, and the wrong way to play the game.

Few guys who had a playground game ever became All-Stars in the NBA. For Earl Monroe, Dr. J, Connie Hawkins, and Elgin Baylor, the playground style was a blessing and a curse. The typical playground legend makes too many turnovers and his shot selection is poor. They're too flamboyant and unbridled. Their erratic play keeps most of them from ever reaching the NBA. The four players I named above had something to fall back on. They had poise, savvy, and talent. They wanted to play in the NBA and they were willing to sacrifice personal glory to become team players.

Most playground legends—even if they were to make an NBA team's roster—wouldn't last long because they are used to arriving at halftime for games. That's when a lot of them showed up for the Harlem Rucker League games. Elgin, Earl, Connie, and the Doc had more focus. Initially, they were blessed to go to NBA teams that could really use their talent. The Bullets wanted Earl to shoot the ball 30 times a game and the New York Nets wanted Dr. J to highlight his playground moves. But when Earl and the Doc won their championships, they had moved on to new teams that emphasized unselfish teamwork.

The playground influence in the pro game today has sullied the fundamentals and team concept of many young NBA players. It has trivialized the hard work and attention to the nuances of the game that are essential to playing the game within the game and winning basketball. Consequently, hardly any NBA player today seems to take losing hard. I don't enjoy watching the NBA All-Star Game anymore. It's become like the McDonald's All American High School Game. The players don't take it seriously. They are out there having fun, having a good time, which is great, but they should play hard and compete, too.

When we played in All-Star Games in the 1970s, we weren't out there to have a good time. We went out to win the game. The players from the East had a dislike for the players from the West. We wanted to prove that we were better than they were. When the first NBA-ABA All-Star Game was played in Houston in 1971, the ABA had more to prove than we did. They wanted to show they were on a par with us. We didn't talk about having fun. We went out there to beat them and we did.

I understand that the All-Star Game has become more of an event than it is a game, but the sloppy play and matador defense seems to permeate regular NBA games. I never liked socializing with players from other teams because I found it difficult to play against my friends. Magic Johnson and Isiah Thomas shook hands, hugged, and kissed before the center tap of a 1989 Finals game, but that was phony. The first opportunity they got, they both hit each other with cheap shots.

When I played, there was separation between the players of different teams. We were over here and they were over there. They don't seem to have those same boundaries today in the NBA. Now everybody hugs one another before games like they're best friends. They gather at center court for group prayers after the game.

I was talking with Bill Russell and Dave Cowens on the Legends Tour recently and they both agreed that there's too much fraternizing before games today. We never did that with the Celtics. We might shake their hands reluctantly before the game, but we never hugged them or fraternized with them before or after games. I used to just shake the hand of Jo Jo White, the guy I was guarding, but I didn't go over and shake Cowens's hand or John Havlicek's.

The attitude of wanting to win—doing everything in your power except cheating to win—starts when a player is young. I used to cry when my high school team lost. I'd walk home alone and wouldn't talk to anybody. When I played for the Knicks and we lost, I never went out clubbing afterward. Early in my career, Red Holzman, the Knicks' coach at the time, saw how much losing ate at me and he tried to console me by saying, "Clyde, the sun will come up tomorrow."

I took the game seriously. It was my profession. My teammates also took losing hard. We would all sit in the locker room after losing a big game and talk about how we could have done something differently to change the outcome. When I left the arena, I went home—or to the team hotel if we were on the road—and I didn't answer the phone. I didn't talk to anybody because I wanted to think about what I needed to do in the next game in order for the team to win.

Today's players don't sit around talking the game out with one another after a loss. Instead, they talk on their cell phones. They talk on their cell phones from the locker room to the bus, from the bus to the team plane. Last year, even after major defeats, I saw Knick players talking on their cell phones. It's not dawning on them that they just lost a game by 30 points? Who the hell are they talking to? Why would they want to talk to anyone other than their teammates or coaches after a loss? Maybe you give a quick call to your wife or your girlfriend, but whenever you see these guys, they're always on the phone. It's unbelievable. If it were me, I wouldn't have anything to say. I would keep my eye on the prize—the goal of winning championships—and talk with my teammates and coaches about what we have to do to change our team's fortunes.

Highlighting style over substance permeates every facet of the game today. Style is an important part of the game and the culture of basketball. Hey, who had more style than Clyde hitting Small's on a Friday night after a big win? But when style replaces substance, when putting on a show leads to losses and shoddy fundamentals, then players need to reevaluate their game.

 **Chapter 2**

DISCIPLINE

I learned early in my pro career that even though the Knicks had a big investment in me monetarily, there was no one who was going to look after me once I left the Garden after a game. At first, I was foolish with my newfound freedom. I never saw the sun come up in the morning until I started staying out late in New York, going out partying. But after a few nights that ended too early the next morning started to affect my play on the court, I set my cutoff time at four o'clock. If I didn't get in by 4 A.M., I was done. I didn't want to still be up at five and six o'clock because it would ruin my day and my preparation for basketball practices and games.

I know four in the morning sounds late, but this was New York City and I was 25 years old and Clyde. Besides, I didn't go out every night. Some nights I wasn't looking to have sex. I was just looking to meet women and get numbers. I picked my spots. I used to start on the East Side at clubs like Fridays, Maxwell's Plum, Titter Tattle, and then I'd end uptown in Harlem at Smalls' Paradise; everyone went up there because they were still open at four o'clock.

The other players would go to breakfast after they went out clubbing. They used to have this place called Wells up in Harlem—across the street from Smalls' Paradise—that was famous for waffles and chicken. At four and five in the morning, the place would be packed. In midtown they had a place called the Brasserie, on Fifty-fourth and Lexington Avenue. We used to make this grand entrance walking down a long staircase where everybody would see us come in. It was all people coming in from the clubs.

But I didn't like to stay out to six or seven in the morning, so after a few of these early morning breakfasts in my rookie season, I just stopped making them a habit. As I said, I hung it up at 4 A.M. and went home and went to sleep and got up around noontime. I believe that the way I approached the game, worked on different skills and conditioning in practice, dieted, and recharged for the next game was a big reason for my success as a player.

The game within the game cannot be played without discipline. Now, that doesn't mean all coaches need to yell at all players. Discipline comes in many forms. I played better because Red Holzman constantly shouted at me to "get on my man." But I also played better because I forced myself to shut it down at 4 A.M.

Phil Jackson and I talk occasionally now and he says the players today have a different mind-set than the one we had. Phil, Bill Bradley, and I all joined the Knicks in 1967. We had each been college All-Americans, but as rookies we all asked one question: "How can I help this team win?" Now players join an NBA team—some coming right out of their high school—and they ask, "How do I get what I want?" It's selfish, and it all starts with a lack of discipline.

The guys today cry about calls, push and shove opposing players, and get into silly fights. Ron Artest totally lost his mind and started a brawl. The players today force shots and lose their cool. I'm not saying players of different eras didn't play undisciplined basketball. How many guys never lose their heads? Even Dr. J and Larry Bird, two great ambassadors of the game, went at it once, throwing punches at each other. Magic and Isiah Thomas too would go off. They got technical fouls called against them, but for the most part, they played under control.

My definition of discipline is for a player to put his team first and to play under control at all times. In 13 years in the NBA, I never once received a technical foul. I think Vern Fleming, who played 12 seasons in the NBA, mostly for the Indiana Pacers, is the only player I know of besides me to have played at least ten years in the league without drawing a technical foul.

Phil Chenier of the Baltimore Bullets once accidentally punched me in the back of the neck—he was trying to strike Bradley but missed and hit me—and the ref called the foul on me for some reason. I didn't yell at the ref or retaliate by throwing a punch at Chenier. I knew what he did wasn't intentional.

Even if he did punch me intentionally, I wouldn't have gone after him. I never got into any altercations on the court. Why should I? I'm not going to act with folly because someone else did something to me. When a player keeps a calm demeanor on the court, it's easier for his ability to shine. The best response to an opposing player's physical or psychological tactics is to keep cool and come right back at him with the force of your game, not your fists. Revenge is always sweeter if your team wins the game. In that game with the Bullets—Game 2 of the 1973 Eastern Conference Semifinals—I did just that. I took it to Chenier and scored eight baskets in a row. The Madison Square Garden crowd got up on its feet and my game ascended to a totally different level where I felt I could do whatever I wanted to do. A close game became a rout and the Knicks beat the Bullets.

When a ref made a poor call on me, I never talked back. I just gave him this look that said, "How could you be so stupid to make that call?" But I never said anything. To me, a look is worth a thousand words. I'd just put my hands on my hips and fix the ref with a look that said, "You stupid guy. What are you doing?" but I'd never say a word. I kept my emotions within. I kept my cool because I knew that I couldn't look like I was losing it. I was the leader on the floor and the other players on the Knicks—as well as Red Holzman, our coach—looked to me to keep my cool.

I like discipline. I like rules. I think they're important, even if players like myself sometimes try to break them. I always had strict coaches. When I was in the eighth grade—when everything would be in disarray on the court and my team started to discombobulate—my coach would pull me over and say, "Frazier, don't lose your head, son. Your brains are in it." It was funny, but I never forgot those words of wisdom.

When Red took over as the Knicks' coach in December of 1967, the first thing he did was fine Bradley for being late to a meeting. Bill was a very punctual guy, and at that meeting where Red fined him, Bill was a scant few minutes late. But Red wanted everyone to know that from that point on, a new strict set of rules was in place. We were captivated.

Red was a disciplinarian. He could tell when things were going awry and he would get nasty. He'd tell Bradley, "Bill, play under control! Don't rush your shot! Block out well!" Bradley could get too wound up and Red made sure he knew his role. Red was hard, but fair. If we were winning, he was amenable to changing his system. He didn't have to have it his way all the time. The only time Red wouldn't let his players have our say is when we were losing.

Discipline and respect were the keys to Red's success as a coach. Yes, he knew the game, and as a former scout he knew talent—he also had the added advantage of having played on a championship team as a player—but foremost, Red demanded that we respect the team rules, our teammates, and our opponents. Red was old-school all the way.

He didn't want anyone to trash-talk or disrespect the other team in any way. I remember one night in a game right before the playoffs, we had already clinched the regular season and I didn't want to play, but Red took me aside and said, "Clyde, you've got to go out there and play for at least a half because the other team expects you to go out there and play. Don't show them up."

Players need to respect themselves first and then give respect to their teammates, coaches, opponents, and referees. They need to respect the fans because without their support, there is no NBA. They need to respect the game and its history. To most of the players today, the league started with Dr. J. Nothing and no one came before the Doc.

Many of them don't know who I am. They don't respect what most of the former players have done in the game. But if they read the record books, they'd have to respect us. The folly of this country is that age is not revered. Everyone wants to be young. But the players today might work harder and appreciate their stature more if they knew about how their forefathers in the game struggled and achieved. It would also help them achieve new levels of greatness.

When a player has no respect for himself, his team, or the league, mayhem will certainly follow. Look what happened to Ron Artest and the Indiana Pacers. Two years ago they had a good chance of winning the NBA championship before Artest erupted. Now they're rebuilding.

Artest had been out of control for a long time. The Pacers tried to rein him in by suspending him but Artest didn't learn his lesson and finally they were forced to trade him. He's doing a great job in Sacramento but you get the feeling he is still a ticking bomb.

Brawling or acting violently on the court didn't start with Ron Artest. Willis Reed erupted one time and fought the entire Atlanta Hawks team, but at least he knew that he was fighting the right guys. And the league was promoting violence back in the 1990s, first with the "Bad Boys" Detroit Pistons, and then with Pat Riley and the marauding Knick teams of Charles Oakley, Anthony Mason, and Patrick Ewing. They were getting tremendous ratings in the Motor City and New York where everyone was talking basketball, but the rest of the country wasn't watching. The NBA television promos back then played up the physical style of play. Chuck Daly and Riley, the head coaches of the Pistons and Knicks, respectively, were hailed as geniuses for instructing their players to play smash-and-crash basketball.

It all backfired when the muscling and bullying became too blatant and there was a backlash from the public. Fans nationwide started complaining about the quality of play. The television ratings dropped and so did scoring averages. David Stern knew he had to do something.

So to counteract the increased physical play and fewer points scored, before the 1994–95 season, the NBA enacted rule changes that shackled defenses—most prominently, hand-checking from the end line in the backcourt to the opposite free throw line was eliminated. The offensive player could move more freely with the ball. In 1997–98, the league enacted more "illegal defense guidelines" to restrict defenders from double-teaming players in the post—only to rescind them in 2001 because not even the coaches knew exactly what they meant.

While the league tinkered with its rules in the 1990s to make the game less physical and to try and increase scoring, it did little to anticipate or curb the escalation of Artest's bad behavior in 2003 that led to the brawl in the stands in 2004.

That incident reminded me of Game 3 of the 1994 playoffs between the Bulls and the Knicks in Chicago when a fight between Derek Harper and Jo Jo English also escalated into a two-team brawl that spilled into the crowd. Harper threw a punch that hit English and then he body-slammed him onto the court and the two players tumbled out of bounds, into the first row of seats. Both teams' benches emptied and the brawl played out in front of David Stern's eyes. He was sitting in the crowd, 20 feet above the court. The television cameras panned the crowd and there was the commissioner looking on, obviously livid. The Chicago fans came to the next game wearing hard hats. It was funny, but there was still the revelation that this is basketball and something had to be done. You can't have the media refer to the game as "basketbrawling."

Rod Thorn, Stu Jackson's predecessor at the NBA as dean of discipline, said at the time, "When it [a brawl] spills over into the stands, you're talking about another level." Harper, a veteran player, knew he had done wrong, and unlike Artest, he vowed that it would not happen again.

"I was provoked, but you have to find a way to use restraint and catch yourself," Harper said, after the brawl. "There was a reaction, which is unfortunate and out of character for me. I don't stand for that kind of stuff, but if you make mistakes you have to learn from them and pay for it. It's unfortunate that I won't be out there when the ball is tossed up tomorrow, but this team has been able to pick itself up from adversity."

That is how a mature, team-oriented player responds to losing control and jeopardizing his team's chances of winning a championship. Harper owned up to his mistake, accepted the punishment, and asserted confidence in his team even in his absence. I haven't heard a similar comment yet from Artest.

After the Artest incident in Detroit, I think the league sent a strong message to the players by levying the hefty fines and suspensions on Artest, Jermaine O'Neal, and Stephen Jackson. Stern called the brawl his worst nightmare and said he feared a player or fan might suffer "serious, permanent injury. It was a horrible scene and it's our obligation to make sure it is not repeated."

I never thought I'd see a player go into the stands again. That's why I was so surprised to see Antonio Davis do just that when he was with the Knicks last year in a game against the Bulls. Antonio thought his wife was in danger from a fan so, without thinking, he jumped over the scorer's table and ran into the seats. Nothing really happened and A.D. is a very level-headed guy but it just points out how important it is to keep working on discipline.

Players who are taught how to build discipline early in their lives—and use it as the foundation of their game— earn the respect and trust of their teammates. Trust amongst teammates and their coaches is an essential component of the game within the game. "[Guys are] going to make mistakes: take a bad shot, turn the ball over," says Larry Brown. "It's going to happen. But you can't compound it by not doing your job, and understanding the trust. I always talk about the trust. If I don't hustle back [on defense] I affect my whole team and I have to believe strongly enough not to ever let that happen." Trust is what separates good teams from great teams. Discipline, respect, and trust are what allow championship teams to climb the mountaintop together and get over the top.

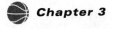

Chapter 3

OVERCOMING ADVERSITY

A lmost every standout player in the league has had to fight through tough times.

All great athletes essentially come to a fork in the road where they have to change their approach to succeed. It's a sign of intelligence and character. My college coach, Jack Hartman, made me play only defense for a full year in practice when I became academically ineligible for my junior year at Southern Illinois. Embarrassed, I thought at first about arguing with Coach Hartman over what I felt was a tremendous slight. But instead I started lifting weights and working so hard on my defense that my teammates hated to see me match up against them in practice. That was the turning point of my life, on and off the court.

In my rookie season with the Knicks, I became despondent over losing confidence in my shot. I felt that I was a jack-of-all-trades and a master of none. But then Holzman and I had a talk. He told me not to worry about scoring. Red said he believed in me and that I should just

concentrate on playing defense. His advice gave me confidence that I could play in the NBA. I settled down and
by the end of the season, I was the Knicks' starting point
guard.

I think my ability to overcome adversity on the court
was directly related to having experienced so much of it
off the court when I was young. Growing up under the
stigma of segregation, I had to deal with adversity every
day. I had to go in the back door of restaurants in order to
get served. I was treated like a second-class citizen. I was
told that I couldn't do that and I couldn't do this. When
you're denied something, it serves as a tremendous galva-
nizer. My parents and coaches used it to energize me. I
developed a tenacious work ethic and never rested on my
laurels.

My parents would tell me: "Walt, people can call you
a nigger. You don't have much, but what you have is your
pride and what you have in your head. You can be whatever you like. Don't take anything for granted."

In basketball, nothing is guaranteed. You can break
your legs tomorrow and never play again. The biggest high
school star—even in today's celebrated youth culture—
might not cut it in the NBA. But I felt that one day, if I
kept working hard, applying myself, and knocking on the
door, I could achieve something great. I wanted to go to
an all-black college in the South, but my mother said that
I should go to an integrated school so that I could learn
more about myself and get a better education.

The experience of growing up black in the South in
the 1950s and '60s taught me discipline. It taught me

pride. It taught me inner strength and control. It taught me teamwork and respect for others. It taught me so many things in life that I still adhere to.

Ben Wallace, who attended a Division II school and battled his way to NBA stardom, has faced adversity throughout his basketball career. "Any time you have to face adversity," says Wallace, "it's humbling and it helps you to relax and appreciate the situation you're in."

Wallace and his former teammates in Detroit understood that in the game of basketball, one player cannot achieve greatness until he learns to subdue his ego and play team ball. This season he'll be bringing that discipline with him to Chicago. Disciplined players who possess sound basketball fundamentals and understand the virtues of respecting the game and the opposition, officials, and coaches, give their team the added edge of being able to handle adversity better. Discipline is what allowed the 1969–70 Knicks to win 18 games in a row— an NBA record for consecutive wins at the time—No. 18 occurring when we came back from a five-point deficit in the game's final 16 seconds to defeat the Cincinnati Royals, and their new player-coach, Bob Cousy.

Every player on our team had dealt with adversity in some fashion. Bradley and I hit rough patches early in our pro careers and had to overcome high expectations and fan and media pressure. DeBusschere had played on and coached a Pistons team that had a losing record in every one of his six seasons in Detroit. Reed had played for three Knick teams that either finished in the cellar of the Eastern Division standings—or second-to-last—before

Bradley and I joined the club. Dick Barnett was 33 in 1970 when we won our first championship, and he had played for three different NBA teams.

When you're up against adversity, when your shots aren't falling, when guys are hanging on you, pushing you, fouling you, and you're not getting the calls, that's when discipline matters. Instead of flying off the handle or blaming your teammates, the officials, or the opposition, players have to keep calm and act decisively to change the tide. Playing the blame game is a sure sign that a team has not jelled and is taking the wrong path.

The young players in the league today have to develop discipline, respect, and control. Amare Stoudemire, before his knee injury, was developing nicely into a disciplined young player who had turned his game around. He couldn't shoot from the outside when he first came in the league, but because of practice and hard work, he had developed a nice little touch on his jump shot and he'd improved his free throw shooting.

Stoudemire is like Alonzo Mourning and my old teammates Willis Reed and Dave DeBusschere. He's aggressive and he makes things happen. He's always hustling and muscling, hounding and pounding guys into submission. Players can always learn finesse, but most can't learn to be aggressive if they don't start out that way. As far as LeBron James is concerned, I think the jury is still out on him. He doesn't have enough of a track record yet to say how he will respond to adversity. Although I was impressed by his inspired play in his first taste of post-season pressure.

LeBron is precocious and seems to know how to handle the weight of being the game's most visible player.

Here he is, a 20-year-old making $100 million, but the guy comes out to play every night. He plays defense, anticipates and gets into the passing lanes well, and he loves to play. At six foot eight, he can create and get any shot he wants. Still, he forces a lot of fadeaway jumpers. He is still developing his post-up game so he relies too much on the fadeaway. Late in games, LeBron becomes tired from shouldering so much of the Cavs' offense he starts shooting with his arms rather than his legs, the cardinal sin of shooting.

Dwyane Wade was magnificent all season long and then he just turned it up even more in the post-season. The way he took over the finals and just buried the Mavericks was inspired. Mark Cuban can complain all he wants about the refs and league-wide conspiracies, but his team lost because they ran into a basketball buzz saw: Dwyane Wade. A lot like my success in the 1970 finals, D. Wade's play catapulted him into the stratosphere of NBA superstars.

Most young players in the league today think they're going to be stars forever because they always have been stars. They think that NBA players have always made millions of dollars. It has all been smooth sailing for them in their basketball lives with everyone catering to them. I think a lot of them take for granted all the advantages they have. They don't know how the league struggled in the past. They don't know how great a position they are in today.

Many of these guys come from tough inner-city backgrounds where they have faced adversity in their lives by growing up in one-parent households and experiencing poverty. But as players, today's basketball culture bends over backward to shelter them from the harsh realities of a demanding coach or being benched for a personal indiscretion. Basketball is not an all-consuming passion for them because they never faced the threat of having it taken away. Everyone holds them in too much awe.

These guys don't want to talk to the press because they hold contempt for any reporter who writes or says anything negative about them. They like the media attention as long as it's positive, but as soon as they're taken to task for mistakes they make on or off the court, they don't want to have anything to do with the media. They will give of their time freely for a story on their celebrity—the houses they own, the cars they drive, and the music they make—but try to find them after a game to talk about basketball, and they're gone.

We used to run to talk to reporters to get something written about us because in the 1970s, pro baseball and football players received much more of the sports media attention than we did. We were consumed by the game and didn't think of ourselves as celebrities. Only if we won championships and fulfilled our basketball obligations did we even think of talking about our lives off the court. We were held accountable for the way we performed in our professional lives and didn't look to shirk that responsibility.

The long-term contracts and youth of so many NBA players today makes it more difficult for teams to discipline these guys. Whenever I talk to Herb Williams or any of the former players who are coaching now, they say, "The young players today just don't know how good they have it." That's why when things go from good to bad quickly, they often don't have the experience in over-coming adversity to adjust and change their behavior.

Many of the players today think the league has always been up. They don't remember that teams came close to folding in the early 1980s, even after Magic and Larry Bird had arrived on the scene. They don't remember that the NBA Finals was played on tape-delay television up until 1982 because there wasn't enough corporate sponsorship interest to telecast it live. The money, the glamour, the attention—today's players think it's their birthright.

Adversity is good. I never knock adversity. Players are not born great. Greatness is not bestowed on a basketball player; you have to earn it on the court in the playoffs. Every champion has to face adversity and learn to overcome it. There have been plenty of players who have had the talent to help their NBA teams win a championship, but it didn't pan out because they weren't equipped mentally to handle the pressure. In the pros, every player has been a star at every level preceding the NBA, so when their role is changed or they have to prove themselves to a new coach, some players do not handle the adversity well.

I'll never forget that in the 1964 NBA draft, the Knicks drafted Jim "Bad News" Barnes with their first pick, the No. 1 player selected overall. In the second round, the Knicks selected Willis Reed, but there were other star college players, like Lucious Jackson, Jeff Mullins, Paul Silas, Wali Jones, and Jerry Sloan that the Knicks bypassed to choose Barnes. The man was six foot eight and 240 pounds, but over two seasons he played a total of 82 games for the Knicks before they traded him. His NBA career lasted only six full seasons.

Bad News had always been a star everywhere he played, but when he came to New York, he had to share the spotlight with Reed. Suddenly, Bad News wasn't "the man" anymore—like they say today. He started struggling and he never got over it. He couldn't handle just being one of the guys because he had always been the star.

His other problem was he liked to party too much. Bad News had a lack of discipline off the court. New York City is not a good place for a young man who likes to party and can't discipline himself and is making real money for the first time in his life. Bad News never panned out because when he faced the adversity of having to share the spotlight and deal with his off-court excesses, he couldn't handle it.

Playing in the NBA of any era tests a man. The players who excel are the ones who have already faced adversity in their lives and know what it's like to overcome it again and again. Larry Bird's Indiana State team lost in the 1979 NCAA championship game after his Sycamores team had recorded a perfect season up to that contest. The following season, he saw his archrival, Magic Johnson—whose Michigan State team had beaten Indiana State in the 1979 NCCA championship game—lead the Los Angeles Lakers to an NBA championship in his rookie season.

Bird did not shrink from adversity. Playing for the Celtics in 1981, Bird rallied to lead Boston to their 14th NBA championship. He played every single regular-season and playoff game that year. Would he have been as great a player without having lost to Magic in the final game of the NCAAs and seeing Magic win the following year? Maybe not. He might not have had as great a hunger to succeed.

Magic, growing up in Michigan, went down to the playground in the winter with a shovel and his basketball. He had to shovel the snow off the court before he could play. Michael Jordan got cut from his junior varsity basketball team. Tim Duncan was a swimmer growing up on the island of St. Croix when Hurricane Hugo destroyed the pool he swam in. Duncan moved to the United States, gave up swimming competitively and started playing basketball.

Every athlete has to stare down adversity before he can achieve greatness. Tiger Woods had to do it. When he first came on tour, he didn't win right away. Then, after he won a number of majors and went through a dry spell, he had to get back on the winning track. Muhammad Ali almost quit in the ring during his first heavyweight championship fight against Sonny Liston—when the ointment smeared on Liston's glove got into Ali's eyes and temporarily blinded him—but he didn't give up. Later in his career, he returned after serving time in jail for being a conscientious objector to the Vietnam War. When he could no longer float like a butterfly and sting like a bee—it seemed like overnight—he gained 15 pounds and adopted the Rope-A-Dope Strategy. It's important for athletes to understand and appreciate history. Not just the history of their sport but of the culture as well.

It's hard to believe but there are NBA players today who don't even know who Martin Luther King Jr. was or Rosa Parks. They don't know about the struggles of Bill Russell in the city of Boston, or that Elvin Hayes was the first black player at the University of Houston and Oscar Robertson the first at the University of Cincinnati.

I couldn't go to a Southeast Conference college to play

basketball when I graduated from high school in 1963. I would've had to be escorted on campus by the National Guard. When I entered the NBA, the league was 50 percent white. Players like Dennis Rodman never would've been allowed to play in the NBA during the era that I played in. Teams back then chose black players first on their character and second on their talent. Only now are teams once again starting to judge a player's character before they give him a multimillion-dollar contract because they have seen, in the case of Artest and other malcontents, how their wild behavior can ruin a team's championship hopes.

When, as a 20-year-old rookie, Magic Johnson had a stat line of 42 points, 15 boards, 7 assists, and 3 steals—filling in as the Lakers' center for the injured Abdul-Jabbar in the clinching Game 6 of the 1980 Finals—he exemplified his uncanny ability to do whatever the Lakers needed in order to win. Only a superlative player with the utmost confidence in his skills and the ability to overcome any obstacle on the court could have dreamed of accomplishing what Magic did on that night.

Building discipline, earning respect, and overcoming adversity are all parts of a winning game plan. If you don't have a game plan, where are you going? When I'm talking about a game plan, I'm talking about how you go about being the best player you can be and how you go about being successful in life.

My mother, Eula Frazier, always said, "Walt, if you're going nowhere, take any road. If you want to get somewhere specifically you must have a plan."

Chapter 4

THE GAME PLAN:
Old-School Basketball

When the Knicks won the championship in 1970, our fans rallied behind us and became our sixth man because they saw a group of five distinct personalities come together and play as one seamless unit. Winning takes a game plan and that's where a great coach comes in. He has to have the vision. He has to be the architect and design a particular style of play that his players can work together and excel at. The great Celtics teams that won 11 championships in the span of 13 seasons (1957–69) never changed their system. They played the same game regardless of who their cast was.

Red Auerbach, the Celtics' legendary coach, chose guys who complimented his three superstars: Bill Russell, Bob Cousy, and John Havlicek. The rest of the guys on those teams, like Bill Sharman, Tommy Heinsohn, Sam Jones, Bailey Howell, and Don Nelson, were just very good role-players. Good teams play to their talents, they play to a certain style, and they play disciplined, relentless games. Last year's Miami Heat squad embraced a lot of these old-school values. Two stars, a strong coach, and talented role players. Guys like Jason Williams and Antoine Walker sacrificed their individual games for the team. And, with Alonzo Mourning and James Posey, they had two tenacious defenders.

When the Spurs won their most recent championship, Duncan and the quicksilver backcourt tandem of Tony Parker and Manu Ginobili enabled the rest of the team's players to fill roles. Bruce Bowen was the "defensive stopper" and three-point threat, Robert Horry was the big shot-artist and savvy defender, and Nazr Mohammed did a little scoring, rebounding, and defended the opposition's big men. The coach, Gregg Popovich, is the disciplinarian who has everybody's respect because he doesn't coddle Duncan.

Ginobili said of Popovich: "He's a smart coach. He knows how to get the best from his team. He's got that temperament that he gets very upset and he's not afraid to tell anything to anybody. He doesn't care if it's Tim Duncan or the player that is on the IR [injured reserve]."

Playing the game within the game to me is synonymous with playing old-school basketball. Many players today think that the game played back then has nothing to do with the way the game is played today. The rift between different generations of NBA players is so complete that in my 16 years as an announcer with the Knicks, only three players—Stephon Marbury, Greg Anthony, and Larry Johnson—have ever approached me to ask me anything about how to play the game.

The NBA has become a player's league. One where

Kobe demands that the Lakers don't rehire Phil or retain Shaq and then hire Phil back; Jason Kidd forces the New Jersey Nets to sign Alonzo Mourning to a big contract; and Marbury demands that the Minnesota Timberwolves trade him so that he doesn't have to play in the shadow of Kevin Garnett.

Learning to share the spotlight with your teammates is a challenge every NBA player—particularly a star player—has to contend with and overcome. There are growing pains in realizing that as a star player, you can never achieve greatness unless you become part of a team. True greatness on the basketball court is achieved by winning championships, and even the game's greatest superstars—Russell, Chamberlain, Robertson, Abdul-Jabbar, and Jordan—never won championships without a good team around them. The star player must slay his ego and learn teamwork and communication skills before he can achieve the ultimate in the sport.

There are different eras and generations, but basketball is still the same. Old school or new school, the fundamentals of the game—passing, dribbling, and shooting—never change. The styles and forms may change, but from 1946 to 2006, there's been a right way and a wrong way to practice and perform these skills and that remains the same. The Spurs and Pistons play old-school basketball today, and, not surprisingly, they win. Miami played a lot of old-school ball last season—playing tenacious "D" and setting up air offensive schemes moving the ball inside out—and look what happened to them.

Winning squads emphasize fundamentals—pick-and-rolls, teamwork, and defense. They play with passion and they play hard. They move the ball, and when their players don't have it, they move well without the ball. They play with sagacity by exploiting mismatches. They gauge their opponents' weaknesses and then attack them relentlessly.

Popovich reminds me a lot of Red Holzman without wearing the same suit. He tells his players, if you don't play team ball, you don't play. If you don't play defense, you sit. I don't care how much you score or how good you are. You're not going to play if you don't play unselfishly and stop your man. Larry Brown has said that his favorite team was the Knicks championship team of 1973 and that growing up in New York, Red was his model as a coach. His Pistons team upended the theory that a championship team must have two or three stars on it. He took a team without a single superstar and got them to win a championship and repeat as finalists by playing the right way.

The foreign players in the game today—Duncan, Steve Nash, Ginobili, Dirk Nowitzki, Peja Stojakovic—they are old-school players. They're all fundamentally sound. They can shoot the ball and they play team ball. They all have one-on-one skills, but they'd rather merge their talents and play unselfish basketball. Nowitzki can shoot the three and post up. Stojakovic has the best stroke from three in the game and gets many easy baskets because he moves well without the ball. They've gotten good coaching as young players. They make their free throws.

The divergence in fundamental skills and team play between the U.S. Dream Team and its international competition in the 2004 Olympics led to the Americans' demise. The Dream Team's inability to shoot midrange shots, play defense, and hit their free throws was their undoing. When I watched those games from Greece, I saw the foreign players running pick-and-rolls, backdoor plays, trapping guys in the corners, and coming up from behind our players and knocking the ball away from them.

The opposing teams won playing sound, fundamental basketball—nothing particularly fancy, but effective. They emphasized teamwork, savvy defense, and exploiting the weaknesses of Team U.S.A. But how many of those foreign players could be NBA players? Hardly any.

Ginobili said about his victorious Argentine team: "I don't think that the national team bases its success on individuals. I think it's an example of how to play like a team, behave like a team, help each other out even if you have that kind of talent."

Brown wasn't the best person to coach the Olympic team because he did not have the right players for his game plan, which involves passing and screening, moving without the ball, perpetual motion. Dwyane Wade said, "There were a lot of guys that were good one-on-one players, and we weren't able to play to our strengths because [Brown] wanted the ball to move around a certain amount of times. You've got guys like Iverson and Stephon [Marbury] who can come down and break their guy down off the dribble. And I'm a good driver. And LeBron. We weren't able to do that." The Olympic game is played according to international rules and court dimensions that are different in some very important ways to those of the NBA. Brown had the wrong players to succeed at a game that emphasizes three-point shooting and versatile big men.

The American team had no shooters; they had scorers. James is a scorer. Iverson is a scorer. These guys aren't shooters. The difference between shooters and scorers is that shooters usually need plays to be run for them or screens to get their shot, but once they're open—guys like Ray Allen, Richard Hamilton, and Michael Redd—these guys are uncanny with their ability to put the ball in the basket. Scorers are going to get their 25–30 points per NBA game, but they're going to take a lot of shots and will drive the ball to the basket to get many of their points. Team U.S.A. also had no defense; nobody could get up on defense and guard his man tightly. In international rules, the defensive man can cause a violation if the offensive player with the ball can't get off a shot or pass within five seconds. But the American team didn't have a single defensive "stopper" on the squad.

It was a calamity that the team was structured for the sneaker companies and not for the Olympics. They let the sneaker companies choose the team. They should have had a guy like Michael Redd instead of James or Anthony on the team. Mike Redd can shoot three-pointers, he can feast with the jumper, but who's Mike Redd? They were going with the big names.

A lot of people think I'm too critical of certain American-born NBA players today, but when you have the opportunity to play for your country in the Olympic Games, young guys like Kobe, Tracy McGrady, Kevin Garnett, Vince Carter, and Ray Allen should not be sitting at home. I know the NBA season is long, but with the exception of Kobe and Garnett, none of the other players had very taxing or long playoff seasons in 2004.

I'm not afraid of the heat or sullen stares I take from some of today's players if I feel my criticism of their play is warranted. Like I'll say during a Knick broadcast, "This guy can't shoot free throws. That's despicable, it's inexplicable." And it is. This is his job. Personally, I think if something is my profession, then not many people should be doing it better than me.

So why should a fan be able to shoot free throws better than Shaquille O'Neal? He's a professional, but you can pull the average guy out of the stands and he'd probably make more consecutive free throws than Shaq can. With the salaries of today's players, they don't need other jobs, like a lot of the players of my era did in the off-season. This is it. So what do they do in the off-season, if they don't work on their weaknesses? A lot of them play golf; they do everything but work on their games.

Young American players for the most part—products of AAU teams with coaches that look to stockpile talent and don't teach the game—just want to go out and run, dunk, and shoot threes. I see six-foot-eight guys who want to be point guards, seven-footers who want to drill the three and that's fine—I'm a believer in developing an all-around game. But give these guys the ball with their backsides close to the basket, and they're lost as to how to create an effective post move that will result in an easy basket.

That's why there are so few good American big men in the NBA today. From Russell, Chamberlain, Reed, Nate Thurmond, Abdul-Jabbar, Elvin Hayes, Wes Unseld, Bob Lanier, and Bill Walton in the '60s and '70s, you have Shaq and a lot of tall, underwhelming players today. Shaq's the only bona fide center in the league today.

What ever happened to the hook shot? Kareem

Abdul-Jabbar scored 38,000 points in his career and many of those came from depositing his unstoppable "skyhook." Every center in my day had the hook shot except for Chamberlain, who was so powerful and tall, like Shaq, he didn't need one. Because of his size and grandeur, Wilt had the "dip," where he backed his opponent in and then with his back still to the basket, he reached over his defender and dropped the ball into the basket. That's why they called him the "Big Dipper."

You'd think a few young big men today would work on the hook shot into their low-post repertoire, but I've yet to see any of them unveil one. The big guys today won't use it. They say it doesn't look cool. But it's a simple shot designed to shield the ball from the defense and get off a shot at close range to the rim. I'd love to see a guy like Eddy Curry develop a hook shot. He has all the tools to be a star in this league but he doesn't have a reliable "go to" move or shot. And it doesn't seem like he's too interested in finding one.

There have been a number of classic shots that have fallen out of favor with today's players because they have been deemed old-school, and, consequently, uncool. The finger-roll is another shot that was used with great effectiveness in my era, but has all but disappeared today. Wilt had one, George McGinnis had one, but George Gervin's was the most impressive. He was so nonchalant about it. He just flipped the ball off his fingertips from five or six feet away from the basket and it would nestle softly over the rim and into the netting. He did it from the corner coming along the baseline, as well as driving down the lane. He just curled it up and flipped it in.

The scoop shot has also disappeared; a victim, I suppose, of its underhand delivery. Larry Bird made a famous one in the 1981 Finals when he lofted an 18-foot jumper from the right side, and as soon as it left his hands he knew it would miss. Anticipating it would bounce off the rim to the right, Bird raced into position to grab the rebound before the ball ever reached the basket, and was in just the right spot when the ball caromed toward the right baseline. He grabbed the rebound on the run with his right hand and, while in midair, with his momentum about to take him behind the backboard and out of bounds, he switched the ball into his left hand and somehow scooped it into the hoop.

It was an instinctive shot. Bird wasn't thinking, he was just reacting. I'm sure he had done that shot many times before in practice—you practice stuff like that, different caroms and where the ball might go—and then he pulled it off in a big game. Today, you rarely see a big man perform a finger-roll or a scoop shot because they want to go in big and over-the-top with the slam dunk.

I perfected a shot that you rarely see today too. It started with me backing down my defender, giving him a head-and-shoulders pump fake to get him into the air, and then jumping into him to draw the foul. At the same time, I would release my shot and try to make an old-fashioned three-point play—a two-point basket followed by a free throw. Today defenders don't play pressure defense the way we used to. They don't contest shots that much so you don't see guys pump-faking anymore. I was very methodical with that shot. Because I was taller than most guards, once I penetrated and stopped, guys went for my fakes and jumped up. If they didn't, I just shot right over them.

The way players pass the ball has changed a great deal too. The two-handed chest or bounce pass that used to be a staple of the game when I played has been replaced by the one-handed look-away flip or throw passes. The alley-oop pass has become more common on the fast break than the bounce pass. Teams are not running as much anymore so the center outlet pass thrown to perfection by an old-school player like Wes Unseld is not as prevalent in today's game.

The guys are stronger today so they throw the one-handed passes longer and with more accuracy than we did. But the best passer in the game today is Jason Kidd, and he is the master of the long, lead two-handed bounce pass. The bounce pass often takes away the element of surprise while one-handed look-away passes lead to turnovers. The players today also love to make cross-court passes that are always dangerous. A big statistic in today's game that was not tracked when I played is the assist-to-turnover ratio. If the floor generals today used more two-handed chest and bounce passes—along with their one-handed passes and alley-oops—their assist-to-turnover ratio would improve and their repertoire of passes would grow.

Dribbling technique has undergone the biggest and most drastic evolution in the game. When Allen Iverson makes his crossover dribble move he carries the ball almost all the time, but in the new NBA, it's somehow not a turnover. I like to see the game officiated according to the rules. The players today carry the ball up and down the court on their dribble and the officials let them get away with it. Even in college I see the officials letting guys get away with palming the ball and dunking from the free throw line without taking a dribble. Palming the ball and traveling is blatant today in the NBA although the league and the refs are beginning to crack down on it.

When I played, the radio announcers used to call the way we handled the ball the "yo-yo dribble." You had to dribble the ball like a yo-yo, up and down. Your hand had to be on top of the ball and the dribbler controlled it not with his palm, but with his fingertips. Now guys are under the ball when they dribble or they carry it on their hip.

If I were playing today, I'd steal the ball from these guys when they go under the ball with their hands because that's when they have less control of their dribble. Once you go under the ball, there's nothing you can do except carry it or pick it up. Whereas with the yo-yo dribble, I could dribble a little quicker—change my pace and cadence—to elude my defender.

Not surprisingly, running my summer basketball camp, I see young kids carrying the ball all over the place when they dribble. I show them the correct way to dribble the ball, but then after I move away and walk around the gym to instruct other kids, I come back ten minutes later and see the same kids making the same mistakes. It's a shame that these 10-year-old kids are all trying to play like Iverson before they've even learned the basics of the game.

Simplicity is the key to a winning game plan that emphasizes playing the game within the game. K.I.S.S.— Keep it simple, stupid—is the Holy Grail to dribbling, passing, shooting free throws, and devising an effective game plan. When I stepped to the charity stripe in a pressure situation, I took a deep breath and then aimed at either the front or the back of the rim with my shot. I wanted to see the seams of the ball rotating as it arced to the basket. Now I see players whirling the ball around their backs, flipping the ball in the air, or taking myriads of dribbles before they get ready to shoot. Just keep it simple.

Cohesion on the offense, intensity on the defense, is the game plan. When a coach puts multidimensional-skilled players on the court who have the savvy to create balance on the floor, move the ball, take high-percentage shots on the offense, and stifle their man on defense, his team stands a good chance of winning the championship. That is what old-school ball is all about.

Old school players make timely hoops at the ends of big games. They have good body control and hands, dexterity is always the catalyst for old school players. They can go right and left when they make their moves. They know when to dish and when to swish and they prosper in the paint. They're not over-zealous in their play, falling into early foul trouble. They're omnipresent on defense, creating havoc for the opposing team. They play under control, not hell-bent, and have a rhythm and continuity in their offensive games. Basketball is a game of momentum and old school players know how and when to pick their spots to make their prolific moves that break the opposing team down.

Chapter 5

THE COMPLETE PLAYER

When I was in college the Game of the Week came on at 2 P.M. and our Southern Illinois practices didn't begin until late in the afternoon—so after watching the NBA game on television and before our practices began, I would go down to the gym and practice Hal Greer's lateral jump shot and Oscar Robertson's ballhandling and back-down moves. With the images from my black-and-white television still fresh in my mind—and the gym empty—I perfected my game by practicing my idols' moves.

Later, after our team had worked out, I would challenge this one guy who I could never score on to games of one-on-one. I'll never forget his name—Clarence Smith—he was six foot six, long and lanky, and weighed like 190 pounds, and he had come to Southern Illinois on a baseball scholarship as a first baseman. I used to hate playing against this guy because when he guarded me he used to just stick on me—the way Satch Sanders of the Celtics did on his man. But I knew if I could get my shots off against him, I could get them off against anyone.

I worked hard to become a complete player because I knew it would help my game. If my shot was off, I could rely on my "D." If I was getting beat on "D," I'd rebound harder and make crisper passes. My coaches encouraged developing these all-around skills but it took a lot of hard work.

The multidimensional player is celebrated as something special and unusual in today's game. A player like Kevin Garnett is lauded for his ability to pass, shoot, rebound, and handle the ball. But these are professional basketball players—they're supposed to be able to perform the fundamentals of the game under pressure. Pretty much every NBA player should be adept at all facets of the game the way a George McGinnis, Bernard King, or Dave DeBusschere was.

Today, the point guard normally doesn't score. The shooting guard doesn't dribble or create. Players are either bred to be playmakers, prolific scorers, defensive specialists, or inside big men. But the irony is that there are fewer quality point guards, pure shooters, defensive stoppers, and great board men and shot blockers in the game today. There are virtually no centers anymore that have great back-to-the-basket games and who plug up the middle on defense.

With the exception of Steve Nash and Jason Kidd, who are the great all-around floor generals?

Today's players are mostly specialists, adept at only one skill. A few years back, the Knicks had both Allan Houston and Latrell Sprewell at the guard position, two

All-Stars, but neither one could slide over and play the point efficiently so it was hard to play them together. When Earl Monroe and myself were the Knicks' backcourt tandem, either one of us could play the point or the shooting guard. If Earl was hot, I became the playmaker. If I was hot, Earl moved over to the point guard position and fed me the ball.

In a game between the Knicks and the Portland Trail Blazers, Portland started two guards, Damon Stoudamire and Sebastian Telfair, who were both under six feet tall. But the Knicks' backcourt of Marbury and Jamal Crawford failed to exploit their height advantage. They stayed outside and shot threes or drove into the teeth of the Trail Blazers' defense. Earl and I would have posted up their diminutive guards and had a field day, but neither Marbury nor Crawford has a post-up game. The Knicks experimented with moving Crawford over to play the point, but he's not so efficient as a playmaker. He's a shooter.

Marbury knows the importance of being an all-around basketball player. Before the start of the 2005–06 season, he said he was looking forward to becoming more of a complete player under Larry Brown.

"He wants me to play the two," Marbury said. "He told me a long time ago, 'If I ever coach you, I'll put you at the two, because you're a two guard.' To me, it don't matter. As long as I'm on the court playing, it don't matter. It don't matter who's the one or who's the two. If I play the two, it's going to be scary. It's going to be kind of scary because now I can shoot whenever I want to shoot and I ain't got to think about that."

Well, that's what he said *before* Larry Brown got to the Knicks. We all know what happened *after* Larry Brown got to the Knicks. For a variety of reasons, that combination of team and coach led to the worst year in the history of the franchise. And there's plenty of blame to go around. Stephon pouted and sulked and didn't always put in the extra effort at the defensive end. He also got hurt. And Larry Brown could never decide on a line-up, he criticized his players in public constantly, and he seemed incapable of adapting his coaching philosophy to the realities of his situation.

In my opinion, the Knicks last year were a perfect example of what happens when you stray too far away from the game within the game. James Dolan, the Knicks' owner, had the highest payroll in the league and he had a lot of talented players. But too many of the players were one-dimensional. There was not enough emphasis on defense and hard work. The coach wasn't stressing the right message, he didn't establish any cohesion, and no one on the team seemed very interested in discipline.

When I played I scored, assisted, rebounded, defended, but how many guards today do you see playing that all-around game? Kidd. D. Wade. Nash. Chauncey Billups can. Gary Payton used to be able to do it. But Tracy McGrady can't run a team efficiently. He dribbles awkwardly. Kobe can't run a team. They're both scoring guards. Ray Allen and Richard Hamilton are also one-dimensional shooters who can't orchestrate.

The one-role system has curbed the talents of the modern player and made him shut his mind down on the court because his job is limited. You don't see guards like

Earl and me or Isiah Thomas and Joe Dumars, who could orchestrate and score as the game dictated and when their teams needed them to change roles. I don't think that a guy like Marbury can make the transition from being a point guard to being a shooting guard. There are no hybrid-type backcourt players today, with the exception of Wade and Kidd and Billups. In my day, you had to do everything. You were expected to do everything and now you're not.

Duncan is another player, like Garnett, who is praised today for being a complete player and team-oriented. He takes good-percentage shots. He's the Big Fundamental. He's fundamentally sound in every aspect of the game. He's never out of control. He's like a ballet dancer. He maneuvers around beautifully in the low post. He has all the moves inside and he uses the bank shot. He plays defense and communicates with his teammates. Duncan is an old-school player. He's a leader.

Nazr Mohammed, who was traded from the Knicks to the Spurs midseason of 2004–05, told me that he was really surprised to see that Duncan was always the first player to arrive at practice and the last to leave. He calls Popovich, "Sir." The guy works hard, so it's contagious. His teammates see their best player busting his tail, and they have to raise the level of their intensity and game.

It takes a great player like a Duncan to break the system and get a team to play with all five players handling, passing, and shooting the ball and playing team defense. It takes a great coach like a Phil Jackson to install the triangle offense in Chicago when the Bulls had the best one-on-one player in the league. The triangle made players like John Paxson and Horace Grant active participants in the offense and much more effective players.

But many coaches still adhere to the system and call isolation plays for their big scorers. As a result, some of the staple, old-school basketball plays—the pick-and-roll, the backdoor play, and the give-and-go—have virtually disappeared in the NBA today. And it's amazing how effective the pick-and-roll still is when teams bother to employ it. Bold coaching tactics, like using pressing defenses, have also disappeared. What ever happened to teams pressing, man-to-man, full-court? Holzman used to say to me, "Clyde, pick your man up when he leaves the locker room." Now you rarely see presses employed anymore.

Basketball is like a chess game. A great team knows when to attack and when to slow the pace down. The key is to assess your opponent before the game—and again as the game is unfolding—and continue to make them play a style that they are not comfortable playing. It takes flexible coaching and players that are versatile to exploit opposing teams' weaknesses.

Playing the game within the game is not about adhering to systems that limit players' skills and creativity. It is about finding the mismatches on the floor and exploiting them until the opponent proves that he can stop the bleeding. Winning teams have guys who can play different positions and know how to sacrifice their individual game for the betterment of the team. A team can't create mismatches when its players are one-dimensional and unschooled in playing different roles. Versatile players possess the instincts and flexibility to sense the flow of a game and make big plays at key times.

Timing is essential. A lot of players today coached in this system which slots them into positions and curbs their playing skills and senses, don't do the little things that win close ballgames. They don't anticipate where a missed shot or loose ball is going. They don't see, when a missed shot hits a certain part of the rim or backboard, where it is headed, the way an Unseld, DeBusschere, or Charles Oakley had the knack for doing when they pursued rebounds. The big men don't see their man moving out to set a pick on the perimeter so they can move around him and deflect a potential NBA championship–winning three, like Hakeem Olajuwon did in 1994.

The system, and the coaches who teach it, takes intelligent basketball players and dulls their innate abilities. There's ten times more coaches today than when I played, counting assistant coaches, but I see players who are less versed in the fundamentals of the game. They make sloppy, precarious passes; they throw passes when they're airborne and not set, the cardinal sin of passing. Many don't perfect the passing, dribbling, and shooting drills they practice in the preseason camps because they know they're not going to get the chance to perform many of these skills in games.

Oscar Robertson was the first flamboyant backcourt man in the NBA, but he never dunked the ball and rarely if ever went behind his back with his dribble. Oscar didn't need to be showy. Just like great baseball hitters who claim they can see the seams of a 95-mile-an-hour fastball coming at them, Oscar saw the game in slow motion. He anticipated actions happening on the court before they occurred. He never reacted because he was always one step ahead of his opponent.

Guys like Oscar and West played under control at all times. They dribbled the ball with control, they made the right passes and always got the shots they wanted. They never made a move if it didn't help them get an advantage over their defender. They were quintessentially old-school, all-around basketball players, both unselfish, but decisive and deadly in the clutch.

There are more Oscars and Wests playing in the NBA today than meet the eye, in fact, there are guys who could probably be better than Oscar or West, but their coaches have to develop their games and then let them run the show. Great coaches prepare their players well and then trust them implicitly to make the right decisions on the court. They trust their players to share the ball and work together. When a team has a coach that trusts his players, and players that have all-around skills and know how to think on the court, then it has balance. Chemistry is another word for balance and you can't win championships without it.

 *Chapter 6*

MAESTRO, PLEASE:
The Playmaker as Orchestrator

When I played in the NBA, there were no point guards or shooting guards—just guards. But every team had a playmaker and, on the Knicks, that was me. I had to shoot, drive, rebound, and defend, but it was also my job to set up everyone else so that they could get as easy a shot as possible. I knew where everyone wanted the ball and I worked hard to get it to them at the right time.

We used to isolate Willis, DeBusschere, and Monroe on one side of the court and then I would dribble toward Bradley in the other corner. I would approach him at a 45-degree angle, giving his defensive player the impression that I would hand the ball to Bill and set a screen to free him up for a jump shot. Bradley would take a step toward me and his man would move out in front anticipating a screen. Then Bill would sprint in the opposite direction towards the basket and I would drop him a bounce pass for a wide-open lay-up. A simple back door cut and it would work most of the time.

You hardly ever see successful back door cuts in today's NBA. Why not? These guys are stronger than we were and they can jump higher and run faster. They could beat their guy back door at will. So, why don't they do it more often? Because there aren't as many confident playmakers out there. Most guys, even point guards, are looking for their shot first. And that's working against one of the principles of the game within the game: Always take the easiest shot possible.

Most of the point guards today dribble the ball east to west, out on the perimeter away from the basket. If I was defending them I would keep them out away from the basket. I'd just keep letting them go over screens, going and coming back out on the perimeter with the dribble, and soon they'd have six seconds left on the shot clock to shoot the ball. How are they going to set up their teammates for an open shot orchestrating like that?

The playmaker's job is not to shoot; it's to create. He has to use his feline quickness to penetrate and create havoc for the defense. When you play the point guard position, you concentrate on everything but shooting. When you do shoot, you need to learn to shoot off the dribble. That way you can draw the defense to you and pass the ball off to your teammates for open shots. The playmaker's role is to be the orchestrator. He's the catalyst. When I led the Knicks' offense or Magic Johnson led the Lakers', before we started a play, we would often direct our teammates to different parts of the court. So we were the conductors with the ball in our hands.

Magic started the trend in the NBA of a big man leading his team's offense, but often the big men coaches choose today to be their playmakers don't have a sense of themselves as orchestrators. Don Nelson, when he coached the Knicks, tried to play Anthony Mason as his point forward, who would bring the ball up for the Knicks and start their offense. Mason could dribble for a big man, but he often dribbled with his head down and he didn't have a sense of where his teammates were on the court. Paul Silas had LeBron start off as his playmaker in his rookie season in 2003, but as masterful a passer as LeBron is, he is not a playmaker because he still looks for his own shot first, and to pass second.

Besides Nash, which guard runs the pick-and-roll effectively today? The pick-and-roll is the oldest play in the game, but most guards today are more comfortable going one-on-one. I see so many moving violations where big men are whistled for moving to try to set a pick. That's the guard's fault. The dribbler has to set up his defender for the pick. He has to take the right angle to his big man setting the pick so that he can come off it ready to shoot or hit the big man rolling to the basket.

Guards today run a pick-and-roll 20 feet away from the basket. You can't run a pick-and-roll 20 feet from the basket. The guard has to position it closer to the basket so if the defender doesn't come out over the pick, the guard can shoot the ball from 15 feet or closer.

The backdoor play is run even less frequently today than the pick-and-roll because players are constantly running out to the perimeter looking for the three-point shot. It is not uncommon to see two or three players in an offensive set out beyond the three-point arc looking to receive a pass.

So many of the playmakers today are shooters first. They do not set their team into their offense early in each possession. Every time up the floor, they're dribbling out on the perimeter for 10 seconds, going nowhere. They are not IQ guys on the offense. The playmaker has to be the coach on the floor. He has to be quick with the dribble so that he can penetrate and break down defenses.

The point guard has to dribble with a purpose. The only way he's going to get from point A to point B is with his dribble. Once he picks the ball up, he's taking pressure off the defender. As long as he has his dribble, the pressure's on the defense. The point guard has to maintain his dribble long enough to set up a play that capitalizes on the defense's weaknesses. Then he has to give the ball up to a teammate in good position to shoot and score.

One of the major problems today in the development of quality playmakers is that the guys who have the potential aren't honing their skills in college. Sebastian Telfair and Shaun Livingston jumped right from high school to the pros. Do you think at 18 they knew how to run an NBA team's offense? Marbury and Crawford spent one year in college. Jason Williams played a total of 48 college games, but he played them at two different colleges over four seasons.

The best point guards today are Kidd, Nash, Wade, Tony Parker, Billups, Gilbert Arenas, and Mike Bibby, who all had extensive college or European professional experience before they entered the NBA. Wade, Parker, and Arenas were all 24 years old when they played in the 2006 postseason; Kidd, Nash, Billups, and Bibby were all at least 27 years old. Their games had matured and they had the confidence and vision to lead their teams.

It used to be that only teenage big men jumped out of high school and into the NBA, but now teenage point guards are entering the league without any—or just one year—of college preparation. As a consequence, many of the floor generals today are green. They don't know how to shoot and when to pass. They don't know when to set up their teammates and when to look for their own shot. They come down on three-on-two breaks and pass the ball to the guy behind the arc for a three-point shot. That's not the time to shoot a three! They should capitalize and go to the basket. They've got the numbers, three on two. But they're passing the ball to a player behind the arc instead of exploiting the mismatch.

Shot recognition—knowing when to shoot and when to pass—is crucial for a floor general. He has to create shots for the good shooters on his team who can't create their own shots. He does this by hitting them with easy-to-catch passes as they come around picks or by penetrating and dropping the ball off to them. Shot recognition and shot creation is sorely lacking in today's game because the playmakers are not properly running the show.

I see these young point guards settling for threes or shooting off-balance shots early in the shot clock. The players are so physically talented today that many of the shooting guards avoid coming off screens because they don't want to run into congestion. They want all their teammates to go to the other side of the court so they can isolate their man, get the ball, and beat their defender one-on-one.

The point guards today can blow by their defenders and create their own shot. But they're not skilled at making easily catchable passes to their big men once they get into the lane. Many of the shooting guards—tired of waiting for their point guard to deliver the ball to them in good shooting positions—beg for their point guard to give them the ball out on the perimeter so they can create their own shot. I see very few point guards today directing their team's offense like conductors, creating open shots for their scorers or themselves.

The reality is that very few playmakers today can consistently hit pull-up jumpers—taking a quick burst with the dribble, making a quick stop, and shooting in one motion—so their defenders slough off them. The passing lanes get clogged as a result and the offensive movement becomes stagnant.

If someone is defending you tight, you have to know how to get your shot off. In my day, there were shot blockers at the basket. You couldn't drive all the way into the lane with Russell, Chamberlain, and Thurmond waiting for you. With all the centers we played against, you had to shoot the pull-up jumper—and once you made it a couple of times, just the threat of that shot made it easier to run the backdoor play or the pick-and-roll.

Quick! Name me three great shot blockers in today's game. You can't. The dearth of quality big men who have the skill to block shots when offensive players penetrate absolves point guards today from having to learn how to shoot the pull-up jumper. Necessity is the mother of invention and the playmaker as orchestrator is the engine that makes a team run smoothly.

Chapter 7

Money, Money, Money

W hen I came into the league, my agent and I worked hard to get the best deal possible. The initial offer we got was from the Baltimore Bullets, who magnanimously suggested that I should sign a contract for $17,000. My agent asked them if they might also offer some kind of signing bonus. "Oh, there's a bonus," they told him. And, when he wondered where the bonus was, they replied, "It's in there." 17K *including* a bonus. That was what I was looking at as a college all-American and the MVP of the NIT. Eventually, we worked out a three-year deal with the Knicks and I considered myself lucky. I've never complained about what I got paid then versus what players get paid now. It's the reality of the business.

It bothers me when people complain about how money is ruining the NBA. Money isn't ruining the NBA. Money is responsible for the game being as great as it is. Unfortunately, money is also responsible for a lot of the game's problems. It's too easy to blame everything bad on salaries. The money is the great motivator. Without it you wouldn't see the kind of individual omnipotence you see throughout the league. One of the reasons why LeBron James is as great as he is is because he wanted that NBA contract. He fought for that shoe deal and for all the endorsement dollars. The bigger the payout, the harder the guys will work to win the lottery.

But the reverse is also true. Once they get that huge payday, it's too easy for a lot of guys to get complacent. It's a sad commentary on the game that LeBron is the exception to the rule: he's a guy who is working even harder *after* signing a huge deal. Too often what happens is some guy is going into a contract year so he suddenly busts his butt and puts up numbers. Teams take notice, they offer him a big contract, he signs and goes back to eating too many cheeseburgers and not playing "D." For a lot of players, the goal of the NBA is to extend your career long enough to cash in on three guaranteed contracts. Then, if you've got any kind of smarts, you're set for life and you have no more financial worries.

And that's all fine. Money is important and, everything else being equal, I guess being rich is better than being poor. But the desire to win is the key component to the game within the game. And just making a lot of money isn't nearly as good as making a lot of money *and* winning. If I had to choose between making 50 million dollars and losing all the time and making 15 million dollars and playing for a winning team, I honestly think I'd choose the latter. Because I've been there before and I know how amazing it feels to work hard and reach that ultimate goal. Also, I'm not stupid; your endorsement money goes up when you win a championship. See? Money plays a role in the game within the game too.

When I entered the league in 1967, there were 12 teams in the NBA and only 144 players. There were so few roster spots that I never thought I was good enough to play in the NBA until my junior season at Southern Illinois when the Salukis came into the old Madison Square Garden and won the National Invitational Tournament. Now 16-year-olds think they're ready for the pros.

The irony is that even with all the young and foreign players coming into the league today, there is still not enough talent to field 30 teams. They have the whole world to get players to fill the rosters of 30 teams—438 players in all—and they can't do it. Even with this blight of talent, there's still talk of expanding. The commissioner cannot stop a prospective owner from wanting to bring a new team into the league when he's willing to pay hundreds of millions of dollars.

Robert Johnson, the billionaire founder of Black Entertainment Television, paid $350 million in 2003 to start a new franchise in Charlotte, North Carolina, becoming the first black owner of a pro team. Dan Gilbert, the online-mortgage magnate, paid $375 million two years ago to buy the Cleveland Cavaliers, even though the team wasn't valued anywhere near that figure. He called it his "lifelong dream" to buy an NBA team. Mark Cuban, the Internet guru, spent $280 million to buy the Dallas Mavericks in 2000 and he sits right next to the team bench every game.

Gilbert sent notes down to Paul Silas, the ex-Cleveland

coach, telling him who to play. Gilbert was like Ted Turner when he first came in as the owner of the Atlanta Hawks. You have these young billionaire guys coming in accustomed to running the show, but they don't know basketball. That's how these owners have grown up; they just buy their way in and manipulate their way through whatever they want. They would coach the team if they could. But they know they can't get away with that.

It's such a new phenomenon in America where a guy can be 30 years old and have a billion dollars. In the 1970s this never happened. All the owners were old and didn't impose their egos on their coaches and players. Paramount was the owner of the Knicks when I played—the Knicks have always been owned by corporations—and the suits were Ned Irish and Irving Felt, who were in their seventies and not seeking any publicity. They were quiet, behind-the-scenes men. Now owners come into the league and they use their teams as vehicles to promote themselves and their businesses.

They want to build championship teams, but they think more about how to make money and how to make the game appealing to the most fans. When Kobe Bryant was accused of rape and every television news show in the country was reporting on the case, Cuban said that it was good for the game because there's nothing more interesting than a "train wreck." He was happy! When Kobe came to Dallas for the first game of the year, Cuban said there would be a sellout crowd to watch him.

When I played, the NBA was a marketing disaster. The commissioners knew little about the game. They were just friends of the owners. They didn't know how to market the game. There were no major sponsors, and little money, fame, or exposure. The commissioner preceding Stern, Larry O'Brien, wasn't even able to get a network interested in broadcasting the NBA Finals live until 1982, when the ratings suddenly jumped from a 6.7 for the 1981 Finals to a 13. Until then, CBS showed the games on tape delay after the late-night news.

Now the game is marketed around the world. Basketball, like soccer, is an international sport in a way that football and baseball can only dream of. The league has done a good job promoting the game in overseas markets. The foreign television rights for the game have tripled in recent years with the influx of international players who have become stars in the NBA. The players are well aware of the money coming in and they want their share of the income. The owners are businessmen. They're not in the business of going broke. They wouldn't pay the big salaries if they weren't getting a return on them.

The money has been a blessing to the players, but a problem to the league's public perception with some of its fans. Many fans believe that the players are making too much money today. The league has prospered under Stern. That's why the owners have given him so much power. He's doing what he thinks is best for the league, and thus far it has worked out well financially.

Because the television contract brings in so much money, the networks dictate to the NBA when to broadcast games and how many games they want on air. The owners push for more playoff games as a way to make more money. In 2003, when they made the first round of the playoffs a best-of-seven series rather than a best-of-five, that was for the owners. Bill Russell told me that the owners don't start making money in the playoffs until a series runs over four games. So obviously, the more playoff series that go to seven games, the more money the owners are raking in.

The players may be overpaid during the season, but in the playoffs, they're underpaid. If you add up what Tim Duncan and the rest of the Spurs shared for winning the 2005 NBA Finals, it was peanuts to what they made during the regular season. All the players and coaches on the Spurs split $2.2 million for winning four playoff rounds and playing 23 games. Divided up, that's tip money for them. So if the players are not claiming a big chunk of the playoff money, it's the owners who are profiting. That's powerful incentive to push for more rounds, more games, and more teams in the playoffs.

Television now owns the sport. There are so many regular-season games televised today that no one game stands out as being significant. The same can be said of playoff games because there are so many of them. If you play once a week, like football, everyone remembers what happened in each game. When we used to play the one nationally televised game on Sundays, everybody just waited for that one game that they were going to see. After watching it, they talked about it all week long until the next game was televised, so it meant something. It was special.

Many of the big-name players today are reluctant to embrace the responsibilities of selling the game. I go in the Knicks' locker room after games and all the guys are in the trainer's room, hiding out from the press. The reporters are standing around with no one to interview. The players do not think that promoting the game is part of their job. They look at it as a burden.

A reporter for a national sports magazine told me that Jordan would give each reporter covering him ten minutes of his time to conduct an interview while LeBron gives one group interview and then he is gone. Guys like Dr. J, Magic, Bird, Isiah, and Jordan saw the bottom of the NBA's popularity in the 1970s and bought into the "rescue mentality" in a way that today's players cannot fathom. They have all this exposure, but they don't want to use it to enhance the image of the NBA and the game.

At the beginning of the 2005–06 season, David Stern instituted a dress code for the players. He wants the players now not only to make more public appearances than they have in prior years, but also for them to look more professional when they go out and make these appearances. The players are rumbled that a sport coat, collared shirt, and slacks would not suit their fashion sense. The T-shirts, throwback jerseys, and baggy jeans that many of them wore would no longer be acceptable under the commissioner's dress code.

"We're working on a job description," said Stern. "The job is not only to go to practice and win games. The job is representing the NBA to all constituencies: community relations, public relations, sponsor relations. Maybe we got spoiled by a generation of players who did these things as a matter of course, and as we got younger, we moved away from them."

Iverson said that Stern's new rules were not to his liking.

"I really do have a problem with it," he said. "It's just not right. It's something I'll fight for."

I think Iverson and the other players who criticized the dress code were overreacting. They're not being required to wear ties, just to dress neatly. They can wear jeans, but not look sloppy wearing warmup suits when they're not on the court. I think it's long overdue.

The prodigious amount of money in the NBA today has had a lot of ripple effects on the game and its players. For one, it has made the media much more aggressive. ESPN has to fill so much on-air space that they search for stories that cast the players in a negative light. This is a real problem. The players' lives are scrutinized and the media is looking for sensational stories that often turn destructive.

We are inundated with details of the players' lives, such as the actresses and models they're dating, what the inside of their mansions look like, and their brushes with the law that are sure to deflect the fans' attention from the game. ESPN sometimes takes more interest in what happens off the court in these players' lives than what they're doing on the court.

I'm personally not all that interested in what these guys do off the court. I don't like watching this "gotcha" and trial-by-media television that occurs on a nightly basis when an NBA star is caught in an infidelity or causing problems at a strip club. It's like when Michael Jordan was pilloried for gambling at Atlantic City to all hours of the morning the day of a playoff game between the Bulls and Knicks in 1993. Leave the man alone. His whereabouts off the court do not need to be turned into national news. The players need to make themselves more available to the media before and after games, but not when the media pries into their personal lives.

I was one of the first players in the NBA to get attention for my off-the-court fashion style and nightlife. But the media attention I received wasn't excessive. People thought the attention I was getting for wearing the fur coat, driving the Rolls Royce, and staying out in nightclubs to the early hours of the morning was negative, but compared to what's happening and being reported on television and newspapers today, I've got to laugh.

Joe Namath and I were criticized for gallivanting around Manhattan, but the stories today about players involved with drugs and alcohol abuse, paternity suits, and rapes make what Joe and I did look tame. We were just two bachelors who liked the nightlife and went around with long hair and sideburns wearing mink coats. The drive by ESPN—and the other cable networks—to get the story first has made the media overzealous. It's changed the fans' focus from the game to all the hoopla.

When the *Sports Illustrated* story "Where's Daddy?", about all the NBA players being hit with paternity suits, came out in 1998, it shone an even more ominous light on the players. Everyone knows today how much money these guys are making and because of that they have to be cautious. My philosophy with women was: "Never mess with someone who doesn't have as much to lose as I do." My first two years in the league, I took on all comers. But when I became more famous, I followed this credo and stayed out of trouble. I chose quality over quantity.

But these guys are targets today and they must be cognizant that the money they make and the attention they receive can attract a negative crowd. When we played in the '70s, pro basketball players were the low guys on the totem pole. We weren't making much money in the sports world, and we didn't receive much publicity compared to star football players like Namath. We had more of a cult following and I never feared anyone trying to get money from me. Today's players have to be very aware of that and it's exacerbated because of how young they are. There are always people thinking that they can get over on them.

The big contracts these guys are signing today are a direct result of all the money the NBA is making, particularly in the past decade with all the provocative marketing. In 1996, the total revenue shared by NBA owners and the players was $1.4 billion. Less than a decade later, the total revenue grew to $3 billion in 2004. It was inevitable that as the revenue from the game went up, the players had to make more money. As the game grows, salaries have to grow correspondingly. The players get paid for the value that they create. Otherwise, there would be strikes, and then no league.

The contracts actually ballooned and became lengthier in duration because of the dearth of talent in the league. The owners knew that they had to lock in the players who could play because with the shortage of talent, if they didn't sign their own good players, some other owner would. It seemed like the prudent thing to do until general managers and player personnel directors inevitably made poor talent judgments and signed players who were not that talented to big contracts. Now teams are looking to reverse that trend because players are not fulfilling their potential and the owners are stuck with paying millions of dollars in long-term contracts.

Although the players' and the coaches' salaries today are startling, they deserve their share of the total revenue coming into the league. The talent in the league is diluted and there are too many teams and roster spots, but the guys that have made it as players and coaches have still beaten tremendous odds in getting this far. Under the new collective bargaining agreement, the players receive 57 percent of the total revenue and the salary cap was raised from nearly $44 million per team last season to $49.5 million per team this season.

The money has gotten a lot sweeter—I was happy when as a first-round draft pick I signed my first contract for $100,000 over three years—and the choices being made as to where to spend all this money have become more dubious. Some of these guys today getting five-year and longer contracts haven't done much of anything yet. The Knicks signed Jerome James and gave him a five-year contract for $29 million when he had averaged 5 points and 3 rebounds for the Supersonics in the 2004–05 regular season and then James did nothing all year. I had to be compared with West and Robertson before the Knicks gave me a five-year contract. But James is seven foot one and he had one breakout playoff series against the Sacramento Kings. The players today know that it's all in the timing. When your contract is up, it revolves around money and potential. When I played, you got paid for what you had proven you could do. Now they pay you for what they think you can do. The league has found out the folly of such a system and they're trying to change it.

But in the new CBA, the Players Association would not budge on reducing the length of contracts. Teams can still sign their own free-agent players to seven-year deals and other teams' free-agent players to six-year deals. Since most Hall of Fame players usually only have eight to twelve stellar seasons, and the initial rookie contracts last four years, that means a lot of teams will end up paying top salaries to guys whose performance level will drop significantly as they age.

There's always jealousy amongst the players over what certain guys are making. It's human nature. But all of these guys playing today should be laughing all the way to the bank. Why should any of these guys be envious? They should be smiling every day. Most of them are multimillionaires. They all should be in a jovial mood when it comes to how much they're earning, but somehow they're not.

In my day, we knew how much everyone on our team was making and we used to kid Bill Bradley—calling him "Dollar Bill"—because he came in as a rookie and made more than anyone else on the team with the initial contract he signed. But there wasn't too much jealousy because even though he was making Joe Namath money, it wasn't so much more than the rest of us were making.

Today many of the players think success is determined not by the number of championships a player wins, but the amount of money he makes in salary and endorsements. Shaq got $27.7 million in salary to play last year, but he was one of the few players out there motivated by pride, and not money. The trade that got him out of Los

Angeles rejuvenated him so he played hard and he played hurt. And he finally brought the trophy to Miami.

Chris Webber and Allan Houston, two injured players who are nowhere near their peak anymore (Houston retired at the beginning of this season), were each paid $17.5 million in the 2005–2006 season. Latrell Sprewell took home $14.6 million and said he wanted a new contract because he had to feed his family. As a result, Sprewell didn't even play last year. If players are coasting or making foolish comments in the media then the league's reputation definitely takes a hit. But a player can't be held accountable for not playing up to his contract if he suffers a serious injury.

When Webber and Houston were at their peak, they were worth the money they got. But Houston developed a chronic knee problem, and Webber is a shadow of his former self. Webber is on the downside of his career. Injuries have taken a lot away from his game. When he was fine, he was a bona fide player. He could play the low post, pass, and hit the foul-line jumper.

When Houston signed his Knick-record $100 million contract in 2001, he was an offensive force with the sweet touch from the outside. Before Webber and Houston started to decline, every team wanted them and that's why the Kings and the Knicks were willing to sign them to such lucrative deals. Usually, the outrageous contracts occur when a player is a free agent and a number of teams seek his services and one team decides to pay the player much more than his market value to land him. You can't blame the players. They're not the ones paying the salaries. They deserve every cent that the owners will pay them, but the players who are motivated by more than the green will excel and become championship-caliber players if their games are as strong as their conviction.

For players like Shaq and Jordan, a team can never pay those guys enough money. Jordan made so much money for the Chicago Bulls and the rest of the league. When he came to Madison Square Garden, everybody made money. All the celebrities came out. Every luxury booth was full. When Michael came to town, money flooded in. He quadrupled everything. It was unbelievable what he brought to a game. Fans came an hour early just to sit, wait, and anticipate seeing Jordan. You could feel the electricity in the air, like a heavyweight fight. All for one man! Shaq's not quite as dynamic, but he's close, as are LeBron, Dwyane Wade, and Kobe. Michael and Shaq both got the game within the game concept that their stardom would reach new heights if they played on championship teams. Their super skills and personalities earned them big contracts and endorsement deals, but winning championships made them legendary players. They also both understood that while making money is important, sometimes a star has to sacrifice financially to help make his team stronger.

Jordan did the seemingly unthinkable by telling Bulls owner Jerry Reinsdorf that he wanted a "loss of skills" clause in his first big, long-term contract. It stipulated that if Jordan's skills diminished, he would be paid a much lower salary. Jordan said at the time, "I don't want to get paid if I'm not the same player." Instead of letting the mega-bucks go to his head and tarnish his drive, Jordan, ever the great motivator, used the money as a carrot to stay hungry. Shaq restructured his contract (less money, more guaranteed years) with Miami last summer so that the team could bring in Antoine Walker, Jason Williams, and James Posey. Without those guys, the Heat don't win it all.

Game within the game players are never satisfied with the amount of money they're making or the number of championships they've won. Shaq doesn't want to stop at winning four. It's his pride, character, and fortitude that is driving him now, not money. It's easy to look back and say how great you were and how much money you made. It's easier to get to the mountaintop than to stay there. Great players do not rest; they don't become complacent millionaires. They keep working.

People ask me all the time if I would have been a different player if I made $10–20 million a year like the players today. I tell them, "I never thought about money until the season was over. When you're in between those lines, nobody's counting what you're making. The only thing they're counting is points and victories."

 **Chapter 8**

The Players' League

In 1967 I flew into JFK airport to become the newest member of the New York Knicks. I was told that someone from the team would pick me up at the baggage claim area. But when I got my bags, there was no one there. I waited and I waited and still no one showed up. By now I really had to go to the bathroom, but there was no way I was going to miss my pickup so I just kept waiting. Finally, after over an hour of sitting on my luggage wondering what was going on, Willis Reed showed up and yelled at me to get my stuff into his car. No apology, no offer to carry something, just, "Hey, Rook, let's go!"

Now I was one of the top rookie signings in the country. A hot prospect who'd just been named NIT MVP. Can you imagine what would happen today if a lottery pick was abandoned at the airport with nothing but some luggage and a full bladder? Man, he'd be on the phone with his agent and his manager and his handler at Nike so fast it would make your head spin. He'd probably demand a trade before he got to the rental car terminal.

But part of learning the game within the game is learning some humility. You sure learned that as a rookie in my day. And an even bigger part of learning the game within the game came from having veteran mentors. Too many players today have outstanding skills that never get developed. They don't have to sit on the bench and watch playoff-tested all-stars show them the right and wrong way to do things. They show up with huge contracts and just start playing. Sometimes they can figure their way through to greatness. But sometimes they get stuck just being really nice players with a lot of untapped potential.

I learned from Willis Reed and the other veterans on my squad during my rookie year just by watching and listening. Whether I was carrying balls or handing out room keys, those guys rode me as a rookie but they also shared their knowledge.

One of the most important things I learned from Willis, I learned on the day he picked me up at the airport. I learned that it's good to be a star in the NBA. Because as Willis drove me into the city in his convertible, we got stopped by the police for speeding. As a product of the segregated South, I was ready for trouble. But the only one who got into trouble was the cop. Willis just started yelling at him, telling him who he was and who I was and how we weren't speeding and we had to go. I thought we were going to get arrested right there but the policeman just apologized and sent us on our way. Willis showed me that if you paid your dues and worked hard, making it in the NBA came with a lot of perks.

When I played, the owners and management ruled the game. Today, the players rule the game. When things don't go right, they want out of the team they're playing for. They force trades like Shaq did in Los Angeles, Mc-Grady did in Orlando, and Baron Davis did in New Orleans last year after he had just signed an $85-million contract extension. They refuse to report to their new team like Jim Jackson did when he was traded from the Suns to the Hornets.

Only Chamberlain, Russell, and Abdul-Jabbar—icons of the game—enjoyed that kind of privileged treatment back when I played. When Kareem forced the Bucks to trade him back in 1975, he didn't go through the media with his request like the players do today. He did it in the off-season and no one knew about it until it came out later.

It's a players' league now. They can get a coach fired or hired, like in Philadelphia where they fired Jim O'Brien when he still had three years and $12 million left on his contract. Rumors were that Iverson and Webber didn't like him. After only one year as the coach, O'Brien was gone. It's symbolic of the "me-first" attitude pervasive around the league. That stuff was unheard of when I played.

Zach Randolph, the Trail Blazers' premier player, was having a tough time adjusting to new coach, Nate McMillian, last season. Randolph was late for the team's first preseason-game shootaround and then was kicked out of a practice for dogging it.

"We are trying to teach these guys," McMillian said, "that you can't do things some of the time. I can't come to play some of the time. I can't show up sometimes. I can't execute my offense sometimes. I can't play my defense sometimes." The "me-first" player attitude change that has been so destructive to the game started to occur when teams became more aggressive in signing free agents in the 1980s. At this time, the players began to fully realize that the NBA was a business and the owners were going to do what they were going to do to get the best players on their team. Players with personal or drug problems in the '80s found themselves without jobs and quickly discarded by teams that showed no loyalty to rehabilitate them.

In 1982, the salary cap was implemented and teams could no longer pay players whatever they wanted. The 1985 Larry Bird exception allowed teams to re-sign their own free agents to allotted salary raises that did not count against the salary cap. That exception dissuaded a lot of star players from testing the free-agent market. It really wasn't until the mid-1990s that star free agents like Grant Hill and Tracy McGrady began taking full advantage of free agency by signing multiyear and million-dollar contracts to go play for the Orlando Magic. Tim Duncan almost followed Hill and McGrady south, but at the last moment he decided to stay with the Spurs.

With more teams competing for a player's service, the owners started catering to the players by using the existing players on their own team to try to lure the desirable free agents to sign on with their squad. But in many ways, that strategy has also backfired. It has become devastating to most teams in the league today that the players have taken over such control now.

When a player dictates what he wants, it's not a good scenario for the entire organization. Some of the recent player and coaching transactions indicate that the league has devolved into personal egoism which a lot of the players are tripping over. For example, Kobe Bryant engineered the departures of Shaq and Phil Jackson from a team that in the previous four years had won three championships and then lost in six games in the Finals and then somehow Phil ended up back with the Lakers but that team is now a shadow of its former self. LeBron James had to approve the new Cleveland coach, Mike Brown, a former assistant with the Pacers, before the Cavaliers hired him and LeBron had all of two years experience as an NBA player. In this case things worked out for the best as LeBron and Brown meshed well. The Cavs made it to the second round of the playoffs and signed their new coach to a five-year extension. But giving a player that kind of juice is still a dangerous precedent.

Alonzo Mourning signed a four-year, $22 million contract with the New Jersey Nets, on Jason Kidd's recommendation, and then demanded the Nets trade him in the first year of the deal. Mourning stated that the reason he demanded the Nets trade him is that the team did not sign Kenyon Martin and it didn't seem to him that they were interested in winning a championship anymore. Coming back from his kidney condition that sidelined him for two years, Mourning said that he only wanted to play for a team that was in championship contention. But he had signed the contract with the Nets, so he should have honored it.

The Knicks never asked me if I wanted Earl Monroe

as my backcourt mate before they traded for him. "Whatever's good for the team," was my philosophy. Today the players want to know who their teammates and coach are going to be. If they don't like what they hear, they force their management's hand to choose different players or a coach or they force management to trade them to a team of their liking.

Kobe wanted Mike Krzyzewski to coach the Lakers after Phil left and called Kobe "uncoachable" in 2004. Why? When has a big-name college coach ever come into the NBA and won a championship in his first few years as a coach? Krzyzewski was wise to reject the Lakers' interest. Why would he have wanted to give up his total autonomy at Duke to play second fiddle to Kobe with the Lakers? And then, after everything, Phil came back to the Lakers and guided them back to the playoffs.

The danger of allowing star players to determine who will coach and play for the team is that it illuminates the conceit running rampant in the league. A player saying he won't play for a certain team sets a bad precedent. The player sits out or doesn't play hard and then the team has to trade the malcontent. It's the fans that get cheated. They don't want to hear about the inner politics of the team and its players. They just want to see players that come out and compete hard every night. They want to see their team play winning basketball.

When I was traded to the Cavaliers in 1977 after having been an All-Star for seven straight years, Willis Reed—my former teammate who had become the Knicks' coach by then—didn't even call me to tell me that I was traded. My agent met me at my apartment in the city to inform me of the news before I heard about it on the radio. I went out to Cleveland and after one year, Bill Fitch, the coach and general manager of the Cavaliers, sat me on the bench. The Cavaliers never accepted me because to them, I was New York. I was always an outsider on that team.

I didn't give any ultimatums or complain. I just played out the final two years of my contract and retired. I wasn't going to tarnish what I had achieved during the first ten years of my career. In that situation, my name and reputation actually hurt me. When my agent called around to the other teams in the league, they didn't bid for my services. I was Walt Frazier. There was a lot of jealousy there. They thought I would think that I was bigger than their coach and their players. Why would they want me around? But they didn't know me. They all thought I was still Clyde.

I felt I could have played somewhere else in the right scenario. But people couldn't accept me being less than what I used to be. They did with other players, but if I wasn't a superstar anymore, the other teams didn't want to be bothered with me. They said, "He's slower," but it wasn't like I had to bring the ball up anymore. They had point guards to do that. The shooting guard had gained new prominence in the game and I could still shoot. I could still play defense and rebound and do all the other things I did before.

Gary Payton left the Seattle Supersonics, and signed for less money in 2003 to play for the Lakers because he said he wanted to win a championship. But then he sulked when he had to conform his game to play with the three other All-Stars on the team. To me, it was a reflection of his character. I lost respect for him. He's selfish. That was the true Gary Payton. He wanted to be a bigger part of the offense. He wanted more plays drawn up for him. He wanted this control and that concession.

I had a lot of respect for Monroe when he came over to the Knicks from the Bullets. All the Bullets wanted Earl to do was score, but when he joined the Knicks he had to be more team-oriented. I didn't change my game at all. I played my same game because my teammates were familiar with my play. But Earl had to make the transition to being a more unselfish player and he did, which I think says a lot about his character.

A player I have a lot of respect for now is Rasheed Wallace. When he played for the Trail Blazers he was a major distraction by drawing so many technical fouls. I wasn't even playing and he was a distraction to me just sitting there trying to watch the game. But he changed when he came to Detroit. He became a great team player. He was a different guy.

What caused the change? He bought into what Larry Brown was trying to do. By playing within Brown's established system, Rasheed saw that he actually had a chance to play on a team that could win a championship for the first time in his NBA career. If most guys see an opportunity to win, they change their game and their attitude from "me-first" to "team-first."

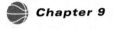 **Chapter 9**

FOCUS:

The Distractions of Sneaker Deals, Agents, and Posses

Back in 1971 I became the first player to sign a sneaker deal. Puma paid me $5,000 to name their newest suede sneaker the "Clyde." Obviously, I had no idea that sneaker sponsorship would become what it has or I would have suggested that they keep their five grand and give me a percentage of sales instead. Heck, I see six-year-old girls wearing Clydes today—and I haven't even played ball in thirty years. But at the time I was just happy to make some money to wear some cool-looking shoes.

I was extremely surprised when the Puma Clyde became such a huge selling sneaker in the New York/New Jersey/Connecticut tri-state area. And, while I didn't make any extra money, the attention I received for wearing a shoe with my name on it didn't hurt my play or my wallet. It didn't hurt Larry Bird or Dr. J or Michael when they got big sneaker contracts either. But these days sometimes big shoe contracts can backfire on a player. Teams have to figure out what's inside a player's head.

They have to ask themselves, "If we give this guy a big contract to go along with his huge shoe deal, is he going to work harder than ever or is he going to lie down and play soft?"

Part of the game within the game is keeping your focus no matter what is distracting you. The great players welcome challenges and opportunities. Your name's on a sneaker? Great. That means you have to go out there and prove to everyone that you're worth having your name on a sneaker. That's what I tried to do.

But there are all kinds of distractions shifting a player's focus away from the game within the game. Take the All-Star game, for example.

The All-Star game has become a showcase for the players to wear their new shoes, making the game seem almost secondary. The latest Nike, And 1, Adidas, and Reebok shoes are sold for more than $125 a pair, often to the minority kids who can't afford them. The shoe companies now sponsor the big summer basketball camps for young players. They sponsor high school and college basketball teams. All of this gives them an easy inroad to influencing young players' decision on which college if any they should attend.

The hypocrisy of the NCAA is that they let these shoe companies control all of these camps and get such an early hold on these kids. Then the colleges hound the top recruits when they're 14, 15, and 16 years old. The college coaches get rich with their shoe company contracts, but the players don't get paid a dime for their efforts and the money they bring in through the NCAA's enormous television and game-ticket revenue. College coaches talk about the free education these young men are receiving, but then they make it harder for them to go to classes and study by adding more games every season. A lot of these colleges play in excess of 30 games a season now and that's not right.

How can you blame a five-foot-eleven teenager like Sebastian Telfair from jumping straight from high school to the pros when before he played his first NBA game, he had signed a reported six-year, $18-million deal to wear Adidas shoes? Now he has to contend with outraged fans at visiting arenas yelling at him as soon as he takes off his warm-up suit because he's the high school kid who got $18 million from Adidas and he can't even shoot a jump shot. It's amazing.

Sonny Vaccaro, the man who signed Michael Jordan up with Nike and had worked for Adidas before he defected to Reebok—which Adidas eventually bought last year—even claimed to *New York* magazine that the Trail Blazers had a quid pro quo deal with Adidas to draft Telfair at No. 13. Adidas has its American headquarters in Portland. When Telfair started slipping in the draft, Vaccaro claims that Adidas was worried that Telfair would be drafted too low and Adidas's investment in him would be tarnished if he fell any lower.

An NBA official who spoke on condition of anonymity said Portland's scouts opposed selecting Telfair with the 13th pick of the draft, but were overruled by Nash. "I have no proof, but in my heart, I believe they made a deal with Adidas," the official said. Two years later, the Trail Blazers gave up on Telfair and traded him to the Celtics.

With the players making so much money and keeping their distance from the fans and media, many of them now travel with a posse composed usually of their friends from back home. Gary Payton when he played with the Supersonics, Iverson, Baron Davis, Kevin Garnett, and Robert "Tractor" Traylor all kept a band of friends around them. Originally, posses were for boxers because boxing is a lonely sport and you need a lot of guys around you. In my era, a player might have one guy with him—whom he called "my man"—like Wilt had his gopher who went in and did things for him. But we never had more than one guy.

The posse scenario is another new phenomenon that I think has been very negative for the players. They're costing these guys money and creating another buffer between players and fans, and in some cases, between players and their teams. A lot of times when people are on your payroll they're not going to tell you what you really need to hear. They'll tell you what you want to hear, but not what you really need to hear. So the players get a lot of biased, self-serving feedback from their posses.

Then the posse's very demanding. They want courtside seats, access to the locker room and training facility, and they begin to overstep their boundaries with the team. They feel that because they're with a player they have clout and that the team has to give them special treatment. I've heard coaches now have thinned the ranks to one or two friends that each individual player can travel and hang out with because of the deleterious effect posses had on teams' conducting their business.

I never had a single guy—much less a posse—hang

out with me. By nature I'm a loner, and then I always re-membered an incident that happened during my sopho-more year of high school that impressed upon me how quickly people can turn on you. It kept me wary of peo-ple who wanted to hang out with me once I became a Knick.

I was the third-string quarterback on the football team, an unknown just learning the ropes, when the first- and second-string quarterbacks went down with injuries. Suddenly, I was thrust into the starting lineup as the quarterback. My high school—David T. Howard in Atlanta—had been a perennial winner in football so when we proceeded to go on a five-game losing streak, everyone blamed me for the losses. It was hard. Only one of my teammates spoke up for me, saying, "We were losing before Walt became the starting quarter-back." The next season, my junior year, I had grown to six foot three and I became the star of the team. The team started winning again, but I kept everyone at a dis-tance. I had seen how capricious people could be and I never forgot the criticism from the previous year. I had experienced how favoritism and jumping on the band-wagon worked, and I wanted no part of it.

Another stepchild of all the money in the game today is the ascendancy in importance of the player agents. The players make more money and have more power than ever today and the player agents have become a more divisive force in the game. The powerful agents can dictate what goes on. Teams cater to them because they know sooner or later the agent is going to represent a player that the team needs. The irony is that the good players should know that they don't need an agent; they're going to get the big money.

It's not always the agent who's able to negotiate the most lucrative contracts. When Grant Hill and Ray Allen negotiated their own contracts a number of years back, they saved themselves the 4 percent commission agents typically receive, and that's a considerable amount of money because they signed $45- and $70-million contracts, respectively. Allen said he negotiated directly with Milwaukee Bucks team owner Herb Kohl because the NBA's collective bargaining agreement sets limits on what players can earn based on playing experience. An agent was no longer necessary in his case.

The best agent is a guy who can get a lot of money for a guy who can't play. Who couldn't have been the agent who represented Dr. J? You sit there and just keep saying no until you get the contract you want.

I became an agent for a couple of years after I retired, but it wasn't for me because it's a babysitting business. When things are going good, the guys don't need to hear from you, but when they start going bad, they say, "How come I haven't heard from you?" It's like having a pretty girlfriend. Everybody's whispering in her ear all the time, telling her stuff, and she starts believing it. I had to tell some of the players I represented, "Hey, man, common sense should tell you that you're not worth twenty million dollars. This other agent is telling you that you are because he wants to represent you just so he can get his fee. You're not going to get twenty million dollars."

I was too honest to be in the business because I wouldn't bullshit guys about their worth. I tried to teach them how to write a check, be punctual, how to prepare themselves for life. Most agents don't want to do that because when the player learns those things he doesn't need an agent. Ultimately, agents want to control you.

Many of the powerful agents today have set out to control the teams. In a few cases, they've forced teams to trade their client because they didn't want their star player sharing the spotlight and the bulk of the salary cap money with another star player. Agents have felled potential championship teams. When Marbury demanded to be traded by the Timberwolves in 1998 after only two and a half seasons in Minnesota, his agent, Eric Fleisher, was believed to have prodded Stephon to leave so that he would not play in the shadow of Garnett and get paid accordingly. Michael Jordan's longtime agent, David Falk, held the competitive balance of the NBA in his hands in the 1990s when his other clients included Alonzo Mourning, Iverson, Charles Barkley, and Patrick Ewing.

Every great championship player has to learn to subjugate his ego and game to another great teammate or teammates. West shared team leadership with Wilt. Russell with Cousy. Reed with Frazier. Oscar with Kareem. Kareem with Magic. Bird with McHale. Jordan with Pippen. No star player ever had a problem with that until today's star players with their egos and agents. Every team was looking for a dynamic duo until what happened with Stephon and Garnett, Vince Carter and McGrady, and Kobe and Shaq. The breakup of these guys was unprecedented and detrimental to their teams.

As Jordan once said, "Some people want it to happen, some wish it would happen, others make it happen."

You're supposed to want guys on your team who can help you win. That's how you succeed. If you get less recognition because you have to share the spotlight, so be it. But some of these guys don't want to sacrifice. They still want their 30 shots. They say they want to win, but if it means giving up something that they're doing, they're not so quick to want to change.

The money and attention have spoiled them. They've had it their way since grade school. Nobody has told them any different. Everybody caters to them. That's the only thing they know. Say anything negative to them and they look at you with a scowl and say, "You don't like my game?"

They take it personally. They hold a grudge. If a coach yells at them, they won't get back on defense. When I was playing, I respected the coach because he was the coach and I knew that he was hired to teach and manage the club. Today you have to be a big-name coach like Phil or Larry Brown to get respect from the players because they don't respect authority figures. And sometimes (like last year with the Knicks) even the big names can't get the job done.

Money is great in your bank account, but when you step on the court, money means nothing. Nobody cares how much money you're making then. Actually, it's a detriment. Because when I played against somebody who I knew was making a lot of money, I wanted to kick his ass even more.

It's like when the Knicks played the Celtics in the 1968 playoffs. We had added incentive to win because they were the World Champions. Everybody was out to beat the Celtics. Players have a similar drive to excel when they know they're going up against a player who is making a lot of money.

When I became a star, every time I stepped on the court, my reputation was at stake. I wasn't going to let anyone score 40 points against me because then people were going to look at me and ask, "What happened?" So it should be more about pride and less about how much money everyone is making as to why players play.

Some guys are bigger stars—some guys make more money—but for that 48 minutes you're out on the court, everyone is the same. It's what you got. What your game is all about. That's what distinguishes you from everyone else when the referee tosses the ball up for the opening tap.

The sneaker companies, agents and assistant coaches are here to stay, but posses seem to be dwindling as teams have set much-needed restrictions on their size and access. Murphy's Law will certainly rear its ugly head when players and head coaches allow too many people to distract them from their goal. Sooner or later the great players realize that if you want to win the game within the game, you have to focus.

Chapter 10

Teamwork and Defense:

The Hallmarks of Champions

I'll let you in on a secret: before I got to the Knicks, Willis Reed never ran hard down the court. Granted that's a big body to lug around but Willis didn't really hustle because there wasn't anyone on the team to get him the ball in the right spot. But when I showed up and started pushing it, he knew that if he ran hard, I'd hit him in stride. My teammates started setting better picks because they knew that if they picked a man off and rolled, I was going to pass them the ball. And everyone started working harder on the defensive end because they knew that if they made a good play or a big stop, I'd reward them with a pass on the offensive end. It got to the point where, if Willis made a block, he'd always race down court because he knew I'd be getting him the ball.

Everyone likes to score. Everyone wants the ball. Everyone has an ego. I guess part of my ego trip was making everyone else's egos feel good. Because a great player who is playing the game within the game has to sacrifice sometimes. Sometimes you have to put the needs of other people in front of your own. And, in basketball, if you're talking about sacrifice, you're talking about defense.

If the Phoenix Suns had won the NBA championship last year, it would have been horrible for the game. No one would say defense wins games anymore. The purists and defense-oriented guys like myself would've died a little death. Every team would've started trying to emulate the Suns by running up and down the court. The Suns almost invited their opponents to score so that they could take the ball out of bounds and start running.

Phoenix's problem was that you can't win a championship by only playing offense. They can't stop anybody on "D." They play matador defense. That's why they traded for Kurt Thomas, a good defensive player, in the off-season last year, and signed Boris Diaw and Raja Bell. It helped, but it wasn't enough. If they had somehow won the championship in 2006, other teams would've adopted their undisciplined, run-up-and-down style and the sweet nuances of the half-court game would deteriorate further.

Defense and teamwork—to me that's the game, that's how you win. That's how I played coming up and I wouldn't change anything. It's still the way to play. I'm old-school. I won't change. I was a defensive player and I shared the ball on offense and hit the open man. I believe in teamwork.

You have to play as a team and you have to work hard on defense. That's how a team develops chemistry. Team chemistry is nothing more than teamwork, working together, camaraderie, and respect for others. Teamwork overcomes height and talent. You win by outworking and outsmarting your opponent.

Good teams play simple basketball. They take what the other team gives them. You pass and go away to set a pick. If your man overplays you, you go backdoor. If he doesn't play you tight, you go over the pick. If your teammate's open, he gets the ball. Simplicity is the name of the game.

On the championship Knick teams, we could read one another. We had that ESP. I had the backdoor and the curl play with Bradley, the give-and-go with Reed, and the pick-and-roll with DeBusschere. There was a harmony that made the game flow and we had five guys who could hit the big shot at the end of the game.

We knew that if we stayed close to most teams, we were going to win down the stretch because we had more weapons. The Spurs knew the same thing when they won their championships. They had Duncan, Ginobili, Tony Parker, and Robert Horry all stepping up down the stretch to take the big shot. The Heat had D. Wade and Shaq. But Gary Payton and Antoine Walker also hit big shots.

General managers today are all trying to find the right group of guys that play well together because they've seen once again in the NBA that success is bred through talent and chemistry. At this level of the game, teams cannot win unless they possess both intangibles.

Jordan understood that when he said, "Talent wins games, but teamwork and intelligence win championships."

Joe Dumars bringing in Rasheed Wallace to the Pistons was a big gamble—a huge gamble that paid off with a championship. Chauncey Billups was the third pick overall in the 1997 NBA draft and languished for years until he came to Detroit. Richard Hamilton was emancipated by Michael Jordan when he traded Hamilton to the Pistons. Bringing in the right pieces—the way Holzman did bringing DeBusschere to the Knicks in 1968—is a very difficult challenge.

Hamilton said the Pistons were so good at facing adversity because they won and lost as a team. The onus wasn't only on one or two star players to win big games. The Pistons have players who look to pass first and then for their own shot second. One player cannot win a championship on his own, but one bad player, if he's not playing the right way, can lose a team the championship, especially during the playoffs when the matchups are so crucial.

Guys like Hamilton, the Wallaces, Billups, and Tayshaun Prince are not box-score players—meaning they don't check the stat sheet at the end of the game to see how they did. These guys have weaknesses, but because they play together with no ego, they're hard to exploit. As well as they played last year, however, they lacked the defensive intensity they had under Larry Brown. Ultimately, that's what did them in against the Heat.

The Spurs have an uncanny blend of offense and defense. They have guards who use dribble penetration to put continual pressure on the opposing team's defense. Ginobili is all over the court and Bowen on defense, hounds the opposing team's best offensive perimeter player. The other Spurs know they can cheat defensively because Duncan does such a good job at protecting the basket.

There's no formula that's foolproof in putting together an NBA team. No general manager knows—no matter what kind of track record and experience a player has in the game—whether a certain player will fit within the design of his team. Rod Thorn is one of the best GMs in the game, but he didn't know when he traded for Vince Carter whether Kidd, Carter, and Richard Jefferson would all mesh together. It's still a work in progress but, to me, it looks promising.

Kobe and Stephon want to put their distinctive marks on their teams, but I think they've both learned that you can't win an NBA championship with one superstar taking over. This isn't the playground where a team dominated by one guy can win. In the NBA, it's easier to defeat a team that relies on one star because in the last five minutes, you only have to focus on that one guy. You only have to contain him. You don't have to worry about the other guys as much because they're not as accustomed to taking the big shots.

If you double-team that one guy and take him out of the game in the last five minutes, who on the other team is going to step up and beat you? The other guys on the team are not accustomed to winning a game with a shot in crunch time. When teams play the Sixers, their strategy is to take Iverson out of the game in the last five minutes and let someone else beat them. As good as Iverson is in getting off his shot under severe defensive pressure, the

Sixers traded for Webber—and his big contract—because they need another star who can step up and knock down clutch shots. With Webber, Iverson isn't the marked man he once was.

When a team plays unselfish basketball, role-players start overachieving. Look at the old Celtics teams. So many guys came to them supposedly washed up: Robert Parish, Bailey Howell, Don Nelson. A lot of these guys came in labeled "washed-up" and then, like DeBusschere with the Knicks or Bruce Bowen with the Spurs, they overachieved. They played above their level because of the team concept. It makes a lot of guys better players because when players are part of the action, they're going to work harder. It's human nature.

When one player shoots most of the shots, the other guys have the attitude, "Well, hell, let him make it. He's taking all the shots." They might not say that publicly, but on the inside, this is what they're thinking. It's the same thing when one guy is making all the money. The other guys think, "He's making all the money, let him do it." They're not working as hard down the stretch because they know they're not going to get the shot. Indirectly, it affects the way they move on the court.

If someone's going to take 30 shots on a team I'm playing for, then when I clear out I'm not going to keep on running looking for an opening. I'm just going to stand around. Again, it's human nature to ask, "What's in it for me?"

A guy running the court with Kidd or Steve Nash knows that if he gets open, Kidd or Nash is going to get him the ball. Whereas if he knows a guy's not going to pass him the ball, he's not going to bust it.

When the Suns picked up Kurt Thomas and Brian Grant in the off-season last year, their coach Mike D'Antoni said, "They'll figure it out real quick that, 'If I get down there to the offensive end, Steve will get me the ball.' It's amazing how guys change real quick when that happens."

That's what I brought to the Knicks in 1967, a backcourt man who would pass the ball and wasn't looking to shoot first like Dick Barnett, Howard Komives, and Emmett Bryant, the other guards on the Knicks back then.

The Pat Riley-coached Knicks never ran plays for Charles Oakley when he played so hard on the defensive end. They took him for granted. Oakley worked hard like everyone else. You always got your money's worth from Oak. The least they could have done is run one play for him and give him the ball.

That's the team game. When Scottie Pippen didn't come out for the last 1.8 seconds of Game 3 in the 1994 playoff series between the Bulls and the Knicks, I was incredulous. Phil had called the last-second shot for Toni Kukoc instead, and Scottie was insulted. He swore at Phil and stomped to the end of the Bulls' bench, refusing to go back into the game.

But you have to be a team player and look at it from Phil's perspective as the coach. Even though the play is not designed for you to shoot the ball, you have to go back on the court after the time-out and play the decoy. By not going out, Scottie set a bad precedent. Guys on his own team said afterward, "Well, Scottie's not with us. He didn't go out." It caused dissension on the team because Pippen was supposed to be the team's leader with Jordan retired.

His teammate, Steve Kerr, said at the time, "I was shocked. The only way to describe it was total disbelief. Here was a guy who had done so much for our team, who had been our leader all year long. He was, and still is, one of the greatest teammates I've ever had. But on that day, I think all the pressure and frustration of our season caught up with him, and he snapped."

When Jordan heard about Pippen's indiscretion, he supposedly shook his head sadly and said, "Poor Scottie. I kept telling him it's not easy being me. Now he knows."

It isn't easy trying to be like Mike. Most people are not blessed with the kind of talent he possessed and they are not as fortunate to have won six championships. Pippen and Jordan had great chemistry together. Other than Bill Russell and Cousy and then Russell and Havlicek, no other dynamic duo in the history of the game has ever won as many championships as Jordan and Pippen. When Michael retired for the second time and left the Bulls, Pippen never won another championship. Maybe he lost his hunger without Jordan. Tim Duncan seems to have that hunger now. He's already won three—two while playing with David Robinson; and now he's partnered with the dynamic backcourt duo of Parker and Ginobili and he looks like he wants to get more rings. But the Mavericks have surfaced in the West, and the Heat, Pistons, and Cavaliers will make formidable Finals opponents from the East.

The teams on the threshold of winning championships recently—Phoenix and Miami—made trades to bring in defensive players. The key player the Heat brought in was Posey. He's a big, lanky, long-armed player who can defend both the two and three position—big guards and small forwards. The Suns brought in more "D" with Kurt Thomas and Boris Diaw. And these moves worked. The Suns almost made it to the Finals and the Heat won it all. It's so ironic that teams that are losing—that are not of elite status—look for more offense. When a team is looking for the last piece of the puzzle, when they're trying to master the game within the game, it's always defense that makes the difference.

 *Chapter 11*

Today's Coaches:
In the Shadow of Red Holzman

I had a lot of trouble adjusting to the league when I was a rookie. I lost my confidence and couldn't score. I felt totally overwhelmed and I really doubted my abilities. But no player alone can master the game within the game. You need good coaching too. And I got plenty of that from Red Holzman.

Red saw how I was bedeviled by my offensive woes so he basically told me to forget about offense. I'm his star guard, the Knicks' number one pick in the draft, and he told me not to even think about scoring. "We don't need you to score tonight, Clyde. Just stop Monroe." And that's what I did. I focused on "D" and shut my man down. After a while of really busting it on the defensive end, my confidence started soaring. And that affected my all-around game. Pretty soon I was swishing and dishing like Red knew I was capable of all along. I finished my rookie year strong and by my second year I was averaging almost 18 points per game.

I honestly think that if I had come up with another coach, my whole career might have been different. There are plenty of players with a lot of talent who never made it in the NBA because they made a bad first impression and never got another shot. Sometimes you need more than hard work and talent. That's a secret to the game within the game that Red taught me.

At the beginning of the 2005–06 season, the top three coaches in the league were Phil Jackson, Larry Brown, and Gregg Popovich, and they all learned the game by watching Red Holzman coach. Jackson played for Holzman and used his key principles to mold his own coaching style. Foremost, that a team dominated by one superstar is not winning any championships.

Larry Brown has the same demeanor Holzman had on the bench—intense but controlled—and he has coached his team to follow Red's dictum: "Share the ball." Larry, like Red, was a playmaker as a player, and they both understood that a point guard must play under control and look to set up his teammates before looking for his own shot. Popovich, a disciple of Brown's at San Antonio, emphasizes defense first and, like Red, doesn't coddle his superstar player.

The best coaches keep their team loose and their advice simple. Before a big game in the playoffs, Red used to pull me aside in the locker room and say things like, "Hit the open man, Clyde. Try to get Bradley a few shots and help Barnett on defense with West." He didn't say anything about how I should look for my shot or score points; it was all about playing the team game and playing defense.

If I were a coach in the NBA today like Red, I would teach defense first. I know defense. It's simple stuff, but many players don't do it. They let players feast on them. I know offense, but I love defense. I always tried to break a guy's spirit down with my defense. Most other players try to do it with their offense by dunking on guys, but they don't look to do it on the defensive end. I never talked to other players or played physical. That wasn't my game. When you try to muscle a guy, he becomes alert. When you stay off him, he relaxes.

If I got all over my man, right away he'd go on the offensive. Whereas if I gave him some room, he'd start feeling relaxed. He's not threatened. Then he starts getting careless with the ball. He goes away from the rudiments of the game. He's not protecting the ball with his body. He puts the ball out in front of his body now. He starts telegraphing his passes. He does all these negative things because I've lulled him into a false sense of confidence. That's when I pounce.

Red would tell us, "When you know how to play defense, it helps your offense." When a guy guards you with a parallel stance, for instance, he has no lateral movement. If you go past him, he has to cross his feet to catch up to you and then he's beaten. It's easy to exploit this weakness by just changing directions and tripping him up. The defensive man has to master the stagger stance, sliding his feet and not crossing them.

If you know the man you're guarding is quicker than you, give him a step and force him to his weakness. I see so many guys guarding Ben Wallace closely when he has the ball 15 feet from the basket and then they give him his right hand. Those are guys who aren't thinking when they're playing defense. They don't know Wallace's offensive game, or his strengths and weaknesses. Wallace can't shoot and he can't go to his left. So why would you crowd him when he has the ball on the perimeter and let him go right? These defenders aren't being taught right. The coaches aren't doing their jobs either. They're not communicating to their players how they want them to guard their men. In general, I like coaches who tell their players this about defense:

"Keep the man in front of you. Don't watch the ball, watch from the chest to the waist. Don't guard your man by looking into his eyes. The eyes can trick you. They can look one way and go another way. But wherever the midsection of a player goes, he must go."

A good coach always emphasizes defense and sharing the ball on offense. Red's genius was how he was always on us for not hustling back on defense. He stressed defense and picking guys up baseline to baseline.

Red took a player like Phil, who was a big scorer in college at the University of North Dakota, and told him, "If you're going to make it on this team, it's going to be through your defense. If you get some offense, use your hook shot. Play within your zone right near the basket and don't try to dribble the ball." Red reached Phil. He made him into a better player by getting him to do what he did best—create havoc on defense.

In 1969–70, three Knick players, Reed, DeBusschere, and myself, were all named to the NBA All-Defensive First Team. The 1975–76 Boston Celtics, with Paul Silas, John Havlicek, and Dave Cowens; the 1977–78 Portland

Trail Blazers, with Maurice Lucas, Bill Walton, and Lionel Hollins; and the 1995–96 Chicago Bulls, with Pippen, Rodman, and Jordan, were the only other teams to place three guys on the All-Defensive First Team since the coaches started to choose All-Defensive Teams back in 1968.

Red made us a stellar defensive team by working on defense all the time in practice. He instructed us. We didn't go up and down the court in our practices. We stayed half-court and played defense. Red was a player's coach. He listened to us, treated us like men, and he was color-blind. He didn't see color. He wanted guys who would play hard. That was it.

In addition to teaching the game and his system to the players, a good coach has to keep every member of his team involved in its success. When Pat Riley coached the Knicks, I was sure there were always three guys on his bench who were disinterested and not ready to play because Riley had his system where he almost never played more than an eight- or nine-man rotation.

But what happens in an emergency when the three or four last men on the bench have to go in the game and play? Why not groom those last three men on the bench for specific roles, like the way Red Holzman had Mike Riordan come in and give fouls? Everybody can't come off the bench and be effective. A lot of players don't have the mentality to come right off the bench and contribute on the floor.

Today, the coaches watch film constantly. There's even a "video coach," responsible for viewing the videotape of games and calling players' attention to pet moves of guys they will be defending, as well as opposing teams' offensive and defensive sets. I think you can get carried away with watching film. When I was a player, we only watched it when the playoffs began or when we fell into a long losing streak during the season. Watching too much film dulls players' senses on the court.

Of course, we also only had one coach. Now there's a minimum of five on every team, not counting the trainer, the strength coach, the video coach, the director of player personnel, the team masseuse and chef, and a scouting staff of around 10 guys, who track the colleges, international players, and the other NBA teams. On the Knick championship teams, Danny Whelan, our trainer, was Red's honorary assistant coach. He kept the stat sheets and sat next to Red and let him know if any of us was in foul trouble. Red never spent the first minute of a time-out conferring with Danny on strategy the way head coaches do with their assistants today.

A lot of coaches today allow their superstar to follow a different standard from the rest of the team. When a team is losing and the players are not doing what they're supposed to do, the coach has to be able to crack down on his superstar as hard as everyone else. When the other players see that the coach plays favorites, it hurts the team's morale. Like Popovich with Duncan, Holzman never treated Willis or me differently from the rest of the players on the Knicks.

A team that plays unselfish, old-school basketball and has moderate talent will always beat a team with one or two superstars trying to win the game on their own. One of the hardest jobs a coach has is to convince his superstar to trust the other players around him. When Phil was able to do that with Michael, championships followed for the Bulls.

Whenever a superstar gets injured, look at how his team responds with him on the bench. Guys who weren't scoring before start scoring. Guys who were scoring score more. Sometimes the team actually starts playing better. A case in point was the Kings without Chris Webber. I thought they always played better without him. When Webber was out they had so much cohesion. When he came back, they stood around. They were a different team with Webber on the floor. They were more effective when everything didn't have to go through him.

Great players must learn to share the ball and make the players around them better. The Rockets don't have any star players besides McGrady and Yao. They have a bunch of role-players. They were lucky to pick up Mike James at the end of the 2005 season—and then they promptly traded him to Toronto in the off-season. He was one of their dominant players because Houston has little talent. But if McGrady passed the ball more and posted up defenders more, he'd be much more effective. The only backcourt man in the game today who has a great post-up game is Kobe Bryant.

The game within the game is hard to master. And even the best players and coaches get humbled by it from time to time. Popovich's Spurs and Jackson's Lakers both had early exits from the playoffs last year. And Larry Brown's Knicks had to endure a real nightmare season, which only got worse in the summer when Larry got fired.

Chapter 12

THE MENTAL ASPECT:

Gamesmanship and Trash-Talking

Dominating the game within the game isn't just a physical task, it's mental too. Everyone always talks about how important the psychological aspect of sports is and that's no lie. It doesn't take much to get you off your game. I remember one time back in the early 70s when I made the mistake of giving two women I was dating tickets for seats that were situated right next to each other at Madison Square Garden. I got so nervous looking up at them during the game—worrying they'd find out about each other—that I couldn't concentrate on my play. I kept making stupid turnovers and missing shots I'd normally make in my sleep. Needless to say, I never made that mistake again. From that day on, I kept the ladies separated.

But little things like that can get in your head and change the way you play. And if you want to excel at the game within the game, you have to know what it takes to psych yourself up and what it takes to psych another player out.

Coaches and players have to know the mindset of the players on the opposing teams and try to exploit any weaknesses they know of in their makeup. For instance, when a team goes up against the Pistons and Rasheed Wallace, it's smart to try to get him to fight himself and argue with the refs. He has a quick trigger and if you can get him out of his comfort zone, his value to the Pistons drops demonstrably.

Rasheed's nemesis is his fragile psyche, and even when he has a cold hand, he'll continue to jack up shots, especially three-point shots. If you guard him tight, you can maybe push Rasheed over the edge. It's called games-manship, and it's part of the game within the game that goes on all the time in the NBA but doesn't receive much attention.

Reggie Miller was the master of driving the Knicks crazy. Patrick Ewing, John Starks, and those guys are still shaking their heads over how he scored eight points in the final 18.7 seconds to win Game 1 of the 1995 Eastern Conference finals. Reggie's crazy to have retired when he did. He should have kept playing. Reggie almost turned into his generation's Elgin Baylor, who retired from the Lakers nine games into the 1971–72 season, after playing 14 seasons in the NBA without having won a championship. The Lakers went on to dominate the league that year and beat the Knicks in five games in the NBA Finals, and if Elgin had played one more season, he would have won that championship that he coveted.

With what Reggie knows about living and playing

the game—plus the tremendous shape he's always kept himself in—he could have thrived for a couple more years in the league. But every player knows there will come a time when the game—because of injury, age, or circumstance, and sometimes a combination of all three—becomes too difficult to play anymore with a passion. Then he must not kid himself and hang on. He has to retire right away. There are no designated hitters in basketball.

I cannot talk about gamesmanship without invoking Bill Russell's name. He was the first master of the art of using gamesmanship to gain the upper hand. He knew Wilt didn't play as hard when he was friendly with an adversary so whenever Wilt and the Sixers came to Boston, the night before the game, Russell would invite Wilt to his house for dinner just to soften him up.

The Celtics used to butter up their opponents by coming up to us during the warm-ups and asking, "How's the family? How's the kids?" Then they'd beat you by 30 points and they wouldn't say a word to you as you left the arena.

Bradley used a lot of gamesmanship in his play. Everyone thought he was the all-American boy from Princeton, too clean-cut to get into any altercations, but Bill was always flexing on the court. He was always annoying somebody like Phil Chenier and then running away. He always had a tug-of-war going with the man who was guarding him, pushing and shoving Jack Marin or Havlicek or Rick Barry.

A compelling part of the game within the game to Bill was for him to vex his opponents. He nagged and annoyed them, but there was always a method to his madness. Bill and Jerry Lucas used to talk gibberish to each other on the court and so confuse the men who were guarding them that they often broke free for wide-open layups. When we knew that Bill had totally frustrated his defender, we actually embellished his ability to disarm his defender by calling more plays for Bill to run his man into screens, freeing him for open jumpers.

Mike Riordan, another former teammate of mine, was a lot like Bill, in that he would do whatever it took to win. Gamesmanship is the art of doing anything within the rules of the game—sometimes stretching the rules too—to distract your opponent from competing at his best. Mike and Bill weren't necessarily dirty, but they were going to test the opposition to see if they were mentally tough enough to endure all the shenanigans they threw at them. There was a purposeful psychological intent to most everything they did.

John Stockton was another player who had gamesmanship down to an art form. He would grab opponents' backsides when he set picks and pull them into him, creating a foul. He was one of the great flop artists in the game, and by setting all those illegal picks and daring players to run over him—and sometimes giving them a little tug to help them—he took countless players out of their games. Dennis Rodman was perhaps the greatest employer of gamesmanship that the game has ever seen. From Michael Jordan to Patrick Ewing to Karl Malone, Rodman unhinged each and every one of them with his flopping and mugging, his hairstyles and fingernail polish. Dikembe Mutombo, at a listed 39 years old—who knows how old he really is—still infuriates opponents every time he wags his finger at them after blocking a shot.

In the 2001 Finals between the Lakers and the 76ers, Mutombo got Shaq so upset that Shaq said after one game, "I wish he'd stand up and play like a man instead of flopping and crying every time I back him down." Mutombo replied, "How can I be flopping if I have stitches in my mouth?" I never cared to use gamesmanship, but some people said that the cool I displayed on the court was a very successful ploy. I lulled my opponents into a false sense of security by staying so calm.

Trash-talking is another way of sidetracking your opponent. Dick Barnett used to say, "Fall back, baby," to his teammates when he shot his jumper to tell us that the shot was good and to go back on the defensive end. But Dick said it mostly to disturb opponents. Red didn't want for us to talk to the opposition. His philosophy was, "Let sleeping dogs lie."

Most of the guys who talked during my day weren't starters. They were little guys who came off the bench, like Freddie "Mad Dog" Carter of the Sixers—yeah, the announcer that you see on NBA telecasts today. That's why not many little guys would come down the lane and dunk in those days. They knew that if they did, the next time they drove to the basket they were going to end up on the floor.

Bird was known for his spicy trash-talking. He greeted the other players signed up for the inaugural Long Distance Shootout at the 1986 All-Star Game with, "Which one of you guys is going to be shooting for second place?" When Rodney McCray of the Houston

Rockets came out to guard Bird in the 1986 Finals, Larry asked him, "You're not really going to try and guard me, are you? What, do you have a problem with your coach? Did your coach do this to you?"

Scottie Pippen could also mouth off. When Karl Malone missed his first of two foul shots late in Game 1 of the 1998 Finals with the score tied 82–82, Scottie said to Karl as he got ready to shoot the second shot, "The Mailman doesn't deliver in the Finals."

Some guys continue their trash-talking off the court, through the media, and sometimes it backfires. Before the Knicks played the Nets and Jason Kidd last season, Stephon Marbury came out and said, "I already know I'm the best point guard [in the league]. It's like asking if it's raining outside. You're going to tell them it's raining?" Marbury held up his end of the trash talk that day by dropping 31 points on 10-of-19 shooting to go along with 8 assists and 3 steals in the game against the Nets, but the Knicks lost the game and proceeded to fall apart for the next two seasons.

The game, when played well, is poetry in motion. Ballet. The amazing grace of a Dr. J or Dwyane Wade soaring like a 747 to the basket pitted against the feline quickness of a cunning defender—these aspects of basketball are why people still care about the game.

But fans and players have much different investments in the game. Most fans go to games to forget their woes. Basketball is nothing more than a contest to these fans. They have a rooting interest, but most of them will only think about the players and the teams out on the court for the two hours that they sit and enjoy a game. For the

NBA player, basketball has been much more than just a game to him for quite a long time.

For the professional basketball player, symbolically and often literally, the game becomes the player's life. He has to live the game to reach the heights he has risen to. He has to sacrifice so much to hone his skills. He might have natural gifts such as height, strength, and athletic skills, but no one has given him anything to get to where he is.

Most fans have never pushed their body to the brink before like NBA players do on a regular basis. They've never faced the pressures of performing in front of thousands of people inside a packed and noisy arena and millions more watching on television. They have no idea of the physical and psychological demands placed on an NBA player. Only other athletes who have performed at extremely high levels can relate to these pressures.

For me, facing and overcoming these challenges was worth it. Basketball was my whole life when I played. I loved every aspect of being a New York Knick. And it wasn't only because I was getting paid. I loved to play. I loved to practice. I liked the physical part—the training, lifting the weights, running the miles, and the sprints in the summertime getting ready for the season; and I liked the mental side, matching wits against a West or a Robertson.

Nothing was more important to me than basketball.

A player participating in epic games feels the heightened excitement, but he can't let it overwhelm him or he won't be able to perform. That's why it is so important for a young player to gain experience playing in big games. When a player has never been in the playoffs, he doesn't know how to prepare for—or even come down properly from—a big game. There's no substitute for experience and maturity to help an NBA player's confidence. The most important lesson he must learn—and today's player may take too far—is how to let the game go in his down time.

He might think he has to change his lifestyle as these big games approach, but he shouldn't change anything. Before my first two playoff series in 1967 and 1968—against the Sixers and then the Celtics, the two best teams in the league—I stopped going out and sat at home all day just so I could think about the game. As a result, I played terrible in both series.

In 1969, during the playoffs I adhered to the pattern I kept during the regular season before a game. The night before, I went out to the clubs—obviously, I didn't go home afterward and have sex—but I stayed out to three or four in the morning. Then I ate the same foods I usually ate, and got to the Garden at the same time—no extra shooting or anything—and I played much better. As I said, there's no substitute for experience and maturity.

The women in my life knew that if the Knicks lost or if I had a bad game, I probably wouldn't be calling them up to go out to dinner for a while or to go dancing. After a big game, I wanted to go out and dance at a club just to unwind from the adrenaline and tension of the game. I remember some people would see me out after I signed my first big contract with the Knicks, and they'd start telling me that I shouldn't stay out late anymore or listen to rock-and-roll music. Then other people would tell me what kind of car I should drive and what kind of house I should buy for my mother. I got kind of confused.

After a while, I learned that it didn't matter whether I was making more money or not. In order to find out who I was and what worked best for me, I had to be myself. I couldn't listen to people telling me that suddenly, because I was making more money, I had to be someone other than who I was. I had to be myself. The NBA player soon learns that the game, the coaches, the fans, the media, and even his own family can consume him if he lets them place their own expectations on him.

Michael Jordan seemed to know this fact from a very early point in his career. After his second year in the league—when Michael injured his foot and was limited to playing 18 games in the regular season and three in the postseason—Doug Collins, his coach with the Bulls at the time, told Michael to take it easy coming back from the injury. Jordan played in an exhibition game that summer and Collins came out to watch him play and told him not to play hard. Jordan ignored his coach and dominated the game. Afterward, Jordan reportedly told Collins:

"I know you're not happy about my playing, but I want you to know something. I just went through the worst year of my life because of an injury and too many people who didn't know anything about me or my body were telling me what to do. They were all telling me what was good for me, but the truth is, what they were really thinking about was what was good for them. I never want to go through that again."

Jordan became so great and had so much charisma that he made fans feel like they were living the game just by watching him play. People who never followed the game, they knew who Michael Jordan was. Even their grandmothers knew about him because when they took their grandkids out to the mall, they all wanted Air Jordan sneakers.

The older people got to know about him because their grandkids told them about Michael. Then the grandparents started following him themselves so they could have conversations with their grandkids. It's human nature. When you know someone, it's more fun to watch him play. Jordan was so personable and he was marketed so much, even the most peripheral fans thought they knew him.

For today's NBA player, it's often hard to separate his personal life from his professional one. They are big targets to a media that has found that high-profile athletes getting in trouble off the court creates big television ratings. If a player's personal life interferes with his business, he will most likely see his production fall and his career shortened.

I've seen a number of players distracted from their job by the relationships they have with family members. I found that I enjoyed being single so that I could focus my energy on my career. I was married in college to a girl I met at Southern Illinois, and had a son, Walt Frazier III, but the marriage didn't work out, and we soon separated. I had not had much to do with women up to that point in my life, but in high school, I remember feeling destroyed when I saw my first girlfriend go around with another dude. I said to myself, "Man, I never want to feel this hurt again."

I never remarried. I liked some of the women I dated.

But I kept those relationships at a distance. I didn't want my lifestyle to be altered in a way that would've taken away from my performance as a pro basketball player. And then I never wanted to feel the pain that I experienced in high school. It was only an infatuation, but I always remembered it. From that time on, I only went so far in love. I never went over that point where I could get hurt. If I saw one of my girls at the Garden with another guy, I took it in stride. I was like, "Hey, I'm not going to shoot at the wrong basket and score two points for the other team over it." I didn't let it bother me. That's just the way it was.

As a professional basketball player, especially playing in New York City, you have to know how to handle yourself amongst a lot of different people. New York's a pressure cooker, but in most cities where there's an NBA basketball team, there's pressure. As a player, you've got to be able to handle the stress of pressure on and off the court.

On the court, when the game's on the line, you've got to be able to come up with the shots. Off the court, if you don't come up with the shots, you've got to deal with the press, the fans, and everybody else who wants a piece of you. You have to try to conduct yourself in such a manner that afterward, these people still admire you. When the Knicks went on the road, the kids who came out early to the arena to see the players walk in off the team bus were even disappointed if I wasn't dressed up in one of my Clyde outfits.

They'd go, "Aw, Clyde, man. We wanted to see you in the mink coat."

Part of living the game in the NBA is dealing with the criticism from the coach, the fans, and the media. As a player, this is a big part of the psychological game. Red would always shout my name. I could be sitting on the bench sometimes and he'd be shouting, "Clyde! Clyde!" Red knew that I was impervious to his yelling so he just used me as a whipping boy. Whereas with Bradley, Red wouldn't yell at him because he knew Bill would only play worse. Red knew the psychology of dealing with each individual player. He wasn't too tough on Willis either, because Willis could be kind of sensitive too.

When we were winning, Red could be loose and funny. When we were losing, Red was a tyrant. His practices became harder. On road trips, as punishment, he wouldn't let us stay in downtown hotels. Red would book us into a hotel on the periphery of the city. It was Red's way of saying, "If you make my life miserable, I'm going to make your life miserable."

When we were losing, instead of showering and going right home after practices, he'd make us watch game film. It was aggravating. He'd say after practice, "Frazier, meet me in my office, we're going to watch film." He didn't care if you fell asleep while watching it because what he was doing was ruining your day. You'd practice from ten to twelve in the morning and then you went to Red's office at the Garden. By the time you got home after watching film, it'd be four or five o'clock in the afternoon and your day was shot. Red didn't care. He had to be in his office, anyway, so he was going to keep you hostage with him.

When Phil Jackson played for the Knicks, he was a maverick. He never wanted to conform to the rules. Phil was a free spirit. I never envisioned him as a coach. I knew he was an intelligent guy, but I didn't think he had the patience to focus on all the details of coaching a pro basketball team. But once Phil got out of the game, he cleaned up his act, shaved his beard, and cut his hair. He did some coaching and broadcasting with the Nets and he realized his passion for the game. Phil learned that he'd rather conform a bit and have the game in his life than remain wild and live without it.

When I came into the league, people didn't know many NBA players by name or sight. They didn't know much about professional basketball at all. It really was more of a cult following back then.

Today, many of the players are celebrities. They appear on television and on magazine covers so much that they have a feeling of invincibility. The money they make further establishes that status in their mind. These players grow up knowing that if they're talented star players, they will get away with many indiscretions. We're all culpable: the fans, the media, and the women have all played a role in making these guys feel invincible because of the adulation we have showered upon them.

It's not just NBA players either. It's athletes in every sport, rock musicians, and movie stars. The stars get special treatment today. Look at O. J. Simpson and Michael Jackson. How many of these guys do something wrong and never pay the price? If Michael Jackson weren't a pop star would he have gotten off? It's questionable. Celebrity works both for you and against you. People say, "He thinks he can get away with everything." So right away, they have this negative opinion of you.

How a player deals with his newfound celebrity often determines his fate in the NBA. My celebrity worked for me early in my career—I was getting more endorsements and writeups than anyone in the game—and against me later in my career. I didn't like my situation in Cleveland playing for Bill Fitch, sitting on the bench. I could have played longer, extended my career, but being Clyde got me blackballed from the game. No other team wanted me because their general managers were afraid that my image would overshadow the players on their team.

By the time I retired, I had lost my passion to play. I wanted out. I was just tired. I couldn't hang around anymore, not even for the money. I was miserable. I started to hate to practice when I used to love to practice. When someone scored on me, it didn't matter. I used to get mad when people scored on me. Because the game is 80 percent mental, there was no reason for me to go on. My mother said to me, "Come on home, son. You've done all that you can do there."

Basketball had been my whole life. When I was no longer playing, when I no longer had a season to prepare for, the transition to leaving the game—even though I was ready to leave—was very traumatic. I loved the feeling of being "in the zone" on the court, like when I was shooting and knowing that I couldn't miss. I would make five, six, or seven straight shots. Everything would seem to come so easy because I was in rhythm with my body and the game.

Later in my career, I started doing yoga because I had

developed a bad back. In yoga, you go inside the muscle you are stretching. When I got into yoga, my shooting, particularly my free throw shooting, improved because I had developed an even more acute focus. Every aspect of my life related to my life on the court, and how it helped or harmed my performance. When I stopped playing the game, I had to search for meaning again in everything I did.

Now that I am retired, I've found that "zone" in other parts of my life, like tending to my botanical garden in St. Croix where I live half the year, sailing in the Caribbean Sea, and landscaping my property. I still have the discipline that I developed as a basketball player. That's why I'm still in shape because the only thing I am not doing today is playing the game. I still watch my diet and exercise. I still get my rest.

Sometimes I'll have these fleeting feelings that I'm still playing for the Knicks and that I'm late for a game. I'm supposed to be out on the basketball court and I'm not there. It's scary. I have flashbacks and dreams of playing games—big playoff games—where I can hear the crowd chanting, "Dee-fense." I have these flashbacks and dreams, but then I break out of them or wake up, and I realize I retired 25 years ago. Then I just laugh at myself.

Down, Clyde! I'm still living the game, but I don't get to suit up in my No. 10 Knicks game uniform anymore, and I sold my Rolls Royce and rarely wear the mink coat.

Chapter 13

TRUST

A while ago I was taking a bike ride through the Upper East Side of Manhattan when I suddenly decided that I'd rather be jogging in Central Park—like I said, I've always loved working out. Anyway, I didn't have a lock for my bike but I saw a Catholic church on Fifth Avenue and I decided to leave my bicycle inside the church. I figured if you can't trust a church, what can you trust? So, I went for my run and when I got back, the church door was locked. I walked around to a side door and knocked loudly. After a few minutes, a priest opened the door. I explained the situation and the priest just looked at me and shook his head. "Oh, my son," he sighed. "I fear you have made a big mistake."

As he walked me through the church towards where I had left my bike, the priest explained that absolutely everything was being stolen from the church all the time, which is why he started locking the doors. And when we got to where my bike used to be . . . it was still there! The priest was amazed although he stopped short of calling it a miracle.

What does this story have to do with basketball, you ask? Well, it's all about trust. I've always been someone who trusts first and will keep trusting until you give me a reason not to. I trust in myself and I trust in my teammates. And that's another key to the game within the game.

I've always thought that one of the reasons why Kobe Bryant shoots so much is because he just doesn't trust his teammates enough. Now, maybe he has a point. Obviously he's a much better player than anyone else on that squad. But Michael Jordan was always a better player than those around him and he trusted them. He always took a lot of shots but he also always trusted his fellow Bulls. Even during the bad years for Chicago when they weren't winning consistently, Michael trusted his teammates and got them the ball. Once he was able to upgrade his teammates from guys like Orlando Woolridge and Brad Sellers to guys like Scottie Pippen and Horace Grant, Michael started winning championships. But his trust in himself and those around him was always there.

Woody Allen said that when the Knicks traded me away to the Cleveland Cavaliers in 1977 for Jim Cleamons, they created a curse similar to the one the Boston Red Sox brought upon themselves when they sold Babe Ruth to the Yankees in 1920 because their owner needed money to finance a Broadway play, *No, No, Nanette,* which flopped. I, myself, don't believe in curses, but the Knicks are in a big salary cap abyss these days and it's making it hard to return to their championship glory days.

I had always trusted Willis. And to this day I don't know why he traded me. I was only 32 and Monroe and I had been the third-highest-scoring backcourt duo in the league the previous season, behind Maravich and Gail Goodrich of the New Orleans Jazz and Ron Boone and Brian Taylor of the Kansas City Kings. The Knicks had failed to make the playoffs for the second year in a row, but we had improved upon our record from the previous season by six wins, and we seemed to be on an upswing with the acquisition of Bob McAdoo.

Willis was not like Red. As the coach, Willis didn't want to hear his players voice their ideas on how the team should play. With Red, you could say anything you liked to him and he listened to you, especially if you were a veteran player. Willis felt more threatened and I think he saw me as a challenge to his leadership.

Sometimes I wonder how differently my life would have turned out if Willis had asked me to help him coach the team. I know I would've taken him up on it because I was only planning on playing until I was 35. If he had said, "Hey, Clyde, play a couple of more years with the Knicks and then help me coach this young backcourt," I would've been delighted. I could have played some and then helped the guys who I knew were going to take over my position.

That is the way I was brought into the game, with older players mentoring me. Michael Ray Richardson and Ray Williams were just starting out then as the new backcourt tandem for the Knicks and I thought I could help them. I was willing to do that with Sugar Ray and Ray.

Williams was one of the most physically talented

guards the Knicks have ever had. He was strong and could jump and shoot. But he was from Mount Vernon, New York—right outside the city—and most hometown players don't do well with the added pressure of family and friends asking for tickets and telling them how they should play. Sugar Ray was very versatile. He could run the offense, score, rebound, and steal the ball.

If Ray Williams and Sugar Ray had developed into a great backcourt—along with Bill Cartwright and Bernard King, who joined the Knicks in 1979 and 1982, respectively—the Knicks might have won a championship or two back in the '80s. King was the most prolific Knick scorer since Richie Guerin, who played in the '50s and '60s. King was head and shoulders above the rest of the players on the Knicks, but the Celtics had the Knicks' number back then.

Bill Russell got to finish his career with the Celtics and Willis finished his with the Knicks. I hoped to do the same. I never saw myself being traded. I knew it could happen because I saw Wilt and Oscar get traded, but I was still devastated when it happened to me.

In retrospect, being traded and leaving New York at that time was a blessing for me. In Cleveland, I had to drop my Clyde persona and think deeply about what it was that I wanted to do with the rest of my life. When I returned to New York in 1989 as a radio announcer, Knick fans connected my leaving with the team's subsequent downfall. That's why people still say to me, "Clyde, come back and help them out." But I would never think of coaching now. For one thing, I couldn't handle the "star treatment" certain players demand.

Perhaps the fans in New York want to see me more involved because they always had a special affinity with the more prominent players on our championship teams. Coupled with the Knicks' descent in the standings after I left, I think New Yorkers held me in higher esteem when I returned as an announcer—more so than if I had stayed with the Knicks as a player and they had continued to lose—because I rekindled their glowing memories of the glory days.

The Knicks now have spent a lot of money on players who have not fulfilled their potential. On paper, the trades they made looked good, but you don't win games on paper. The problem with the Knicks last season was that they didn't have a shot blocker in the lane or a guard who could defend on the perimeter. Guards I never heard of before had career games against the Knicks. Every night, it was a different guard. The Knicks couldn't stop anyone. A good defensive team doesn't let that happen.

The Knicks still need defensive stoppers more than they need offense. Without a shot blocker, every night guys are driving the paint.

Isiah tried to address that problem by picking up two big men: Eddy Curry and Jerome James. But James was overweight and overrated and Curry is still in his NBA infancy, learning how to play this game at the highest level.

The Knicks still need a guy who can defend at the guard position. Crawford can't do it, although he was definitely the most improved Knick last year. Stephon can't do it. They need a Shandon Anderson–type guy: big, athletic, and can play the two guard and defend. The

Knicks criticized Anderson for not being a good shooter, but that's not his game. They got upset with him in the 2004 playoffs because he couldn't score. Then they got rid of him. That's New York. It's not a coincidence that the team Shandon ended up on, the Miami Heat, won it all last year while the Knicks were mired in futility.

The money is irrelevant in New York. Last summer's coaching craziness proves that. The Dolan family wants to win. That's what New York is all about. Everything in New York is more expensive. The owners will pay anything for a championship. But they have to make a decision whether they want to continue to try to buy a team or build one through the draft. And, most importantly, they'll have to decide who to trust.

Chapter 14

RACE IN THE GAME

When I was in high school, football was my main sport. I was the star quarterback at David T. Howard High in Atlanta, Georgia, and I loved it. Sure, I liked basketball too but football was my passion. But when I headed to college I started thinking about what I was going to do for the rest of my life. I looked around at big time colleges and all the pro teams and there really weren't any black quarterbacks out there. I had no role models to follow so I ended up turning my back on football and just playing basketball. Obviously everything turned out for the best. I wouldn't want to be hobbling around today on busted-up knees like Broadway Joe. But it points out that, for better or worse, race plays a part in everything we do—even in the game within the game. As Red Holzman taught us, if you really want to excel at the highest level, you have to trust your teammates, your coaches, and yourself. He taught his players to be just like him: color blind.

But the NBA doesn't always live up to the high standards of guys like Red. And issues of race are still omnipresent in our league.

When Steve Nash won the Most Valuable Player Award two years running, it was unprecedented. He never averaged more than 19 points per game. The writers who voted for Nash over Shaquille O'Neal and Le-Bron James and Kobe Bryant opened up a Pandora's box. No one has ever won the MVP with the statistics that Nash had.

I don't know if racism had anything to do with the voting. I just don't think Nash should have won the MVP over Shaq two years ago, and I would have given it to LeBron last season. It will lead to a lot of accusations of racism and scrutiny in the future if a black player propels his team to a very good season while tallying mediocre personal numbers and he does not win the MVP. People are going to say it's racist that Nash won the award and not this black player who basically had the same type of season.

What the 60-or-so voters—mostly newspaper and magazine NBA beat writers—did by naming Nash the MVP is totally counter to how the voting has gone since 1956, when the NBA selected its first MVP. Bob Cousy, a small white point guard, won the award in 1957 when the Celtics won their second championship, but Cousy averaged 20.6 points per game and 7.5 assists. And that was when recording an assist was much more difficult than it is today, because back then a pass had to lead directly to the scoring of a basket, which is not so today. The only other conventional point guard to win the

MVP was Oscar Robertson in 1963–64 when he averaged 31.4 points per game, 11 assists, and 10 rebounds. The closest I ever came in the voting to winning the MVP was fourth. In 1969–70, when the Knicks won our first championship, I averaged nearly 21 points per game on 51.8 percent shooting and dished off for more than 8 assists per game and rebounded and defended, but I wasn't going to beat out Abdul-Jabbar, Chamberlain, and Reed. Only seven non–big men have ever won the MVP in the 50-year history of the award: Cousy, Oscar, Bird, Magic, Michael, Iverson, and Nash. Only six white players have ever won the MVP: Bob Pettit (twice), Cousy, Bill Walton, Dave Cowens, Bird (three times), and now Nash twice.

Racism exists in the NBA even though the players are 80 percent black. The league is light years ahead of the other professional sports leagues as far as the number of black coaches and general managers. And I was pleased to see that Avery Johnson won Coach of the Year last season.

When I travel around, I see very few of my peers—former players—that are doing anything in the league. These are guys who built the game up in the years that it wasn't very popular and now they can't even get jobs as scouts. I know Nate Archibald would love to coach. He coached at the NBA developmental level and didn't have success, but he would make a great scout or assistant coach for an NBA team. It seems like Nate and so many others like him have been ostracized from the league for some reason. I would like to see an adequate number of black former players profit from the game.

What I find equally troubling is the public's perception of black pro basketball players. Most fans don't believe the black players with big contracts deserve the millions of dollars they are making. The first thing I hear coming out of many people's mouths when a black player signs a multimillion-dollar contract is, "What's he going to do with all that money?" No one asks Donald Trump what he's going to do with all the money he has—and his dad staked him to the initial money he had. No one gave these black NBA players anything. They worked hard to get to the top of their sport.

Rock stars and movie actors make outrageous amounts of money, but I never hear people ask what the Rolling Stones or Tom Hanks do with their money. A lot of people will even ask me, when a black player signs a big contract, "What's he going to do with all that money?" As if I would share this point of view.

I don't think the people who ask this question are aware that they're making a racist comment. But it is racist to single out black basketball players for the money they make and to imply that because they might come from poor beginnings, they won't know how to spend all the money they're earning. I don't hear the same people asking me what Peyton Manning, Roger Clemens, or Phil Jackson is going to do with all the money they're making.

Even Russ Granik, the former deputy commissioner of the NBA, implied that Billy Hunter, the black executive director of the Players Association, was a pawn to the agents, who are mostly white, and, according to Granik, were actually running the show. Granik said that the reason the collective bargaining agreement between the league and the players had initially broken down last summer was because the agents had told Hunter not to accept the terms, especially in regard to reducing the number of years for which teams can sign a player to a long-term contract.

Hunter said, "The inference is that me, as a black man, cannot operate an institution such as the Union without having some white men oversee and legitimize whatever it is I'm supposed to be doing."

These are issues and gaffes that arise because, though the players are 80 percent black, the fans who come out to the arenas are 90 percent white. The NBA, the fans, the media—which is also mostly white—are still looking for the Great White Hope in basketball. They have to. It's a surreal revelation that there are so few white players in the league today and the fans still support the game. For the most part, they've just accepted the racial imbalance of the players as a fact.

Larry Bird realizes the importance of a great white American star in the sport today.

"When I played," Bird said, "you had me and Kevin [McHale] and some others throughout the league. I think it's good for a fan base because, as we all know, the majority of the fans are white America. And if you just had a couple of white guys in there, you might get them a little excited. But it is a black man's game, and it will be forever. I mean, the greatest athletes in the world are African American."

I remember not too long ago when it was unthinkable for a team to field an entire black starting five. But now that happens all the time.

Who are the white American stars in the game today? Keith Van Horn? Wally Szczerbiak? Mike Miller? Jason Williams? Kirk Hinrich? Mike Dunleavy? Raef LaFrentz? No fan is going to forget George Mikan, Bob Cousy, Bob Pettit, Dolph Schayes, Dave DeBusschere, Rick Barry, Bird, McHale, Chris Mullin, or John Stockton watching these guys play.

The NBA is looking for the next Great White American Hope and so am I. I'm looking for the next Larry Bird to come into the league. It was supposed to be Danny Ferry in 1990, then Christian Laettner in 1992, then Van Horn in 1997, and finally Mike Dunleavy in 2002, but none of these guys has had a standout professional career. Fans want to see white American players excel in a predominantly black sport whether it's basketball or boxing. Remember the excitement Gerry Cooney created in the heavyweight ranks in the 1980s when he fought Larry Holmes for the title? Two of the best college players in the game last year were Gonzaga's Adam Morrison and Duke's JJ Redick. When they enter the league this season they will be cast as the next Great White American Hopes.

Will American fans embrace foreign white players with names like Emanuel Ginobili and Dirk Nowitzki? I don't think so, although Dirk certainly won over a lot of fans with his vivacious performance in the playoffs. Where is the next Great White American Hope? A lot are whiling away afternoons on their computers playing video games. The gym rat is a dying breed in America.

There are certain cities that seem to benefit at the arena gate more than others by having a white star. Until recently, Boston always had a white player who starred on the team. Denver also sought star white players like Dan Issel and Kiki Vandeweghe. Phoenix, Utah, and Sacramento are other cities that have always had a star white player. When the Celtics were winning all those championships in the 1950s and '60s with Bill Russell as their star, they never sold out the Boston Garden. They didn't start selling out in Boston until Bird got there.

Russell may not have been the most fan-friendly player, but neither was Bird. Russell always claimed that he would have been more popular if he were white. The big baseball and hockey stars in Boston in the 1960s were white, Bobby Orr and Carl Yastrzemski, and Russell lamented that they received much more fanfare than he did. That is why he refused to return to Boston for many years after his retirement. The black fans in Boston understood that and lived with it. In the 1980s, when the Celtics played the Sixers in big playoff games at Boston Garden, most of the black fans in Boston rooted for Dr. J and the Sixers instead of their hometown team.

In 1950, Nat "Sweetwater" Clifton became the first black player to sign an NBA contract. Clifton, who had played for years with the Harlem Globetrotters, then became the first black player in an NBA game as a member of the Knicks. Later that same season, Chuck Cooper, Earl Lloyd, and Hank DeZonie also played in the NBA. Known as the "Big Four," Clifton, Cooper of the Celtics, Lloyd of the Washington Capitols, and DeZonie of the Tri-Cities Hawks, respectively, became NBA players three years after Jackie Robinson broke the color barrier in Major League Baseball.

But like I said, the league was about 50 percent white in 1967 when I broke in. We used to walk through airports and because we had a number of black players on the Knicks—Willis, Barnett, Dave Stallworth, Cazzie, Nate Bowman, John Warren, and myself—people used to ask us if we were the Harlem Globetrotters.

New Yorkers like style, so between the two of us, Willis and I became the first cross-race stars in New York. The other sports stars in the city in those days—Joe Namath, Tom Seaver, Bradley, and DeBusschere—were all white. The celebrity fans in our day were not black like Spike Lee, Denzel Washington, and Samuel L. Jackson. They were white celebrities like Robert Redford, Dustin Hoffman, and Woody Allen.

Now two of the most popular players in the league with both young black and white fans are Allen Iverson and Stephon Marbury. Both these guys' jerseys are in the top 10 sold amongst NBA players. The controversial players are the ones most revered today. They make the most money. A guy like Duncan never gets in any trouble and nobody cares about him. He's too goody-two-shoes. It's like what they said about Kobe before his problems, "He's too good. He doesn't have enough street cred to sell basketball shoes."

It's Iverson the corporations and the NBA promote. Reebok has pumped his shoe, the "Answer," since his career started with commercials showing him riding around inner-city neighborhoods with his cronies. This guy with his tattoos, gold chains, and avowed disdain for practicing, that's who they want your kids to revere and idolize. That kind of guy, if he played back in the '70s, would have been ostracized.

But, truthfully, I think it's good. Corporate America no longer sees black and white. They just see green now—what makes them money. The business of basketball can sometimes be at odds with the game of basketball. And it's not like race is no longer an issue in our sport. But compared to the racial woes in the rest of society, the basketball world is doing pretty well.

There are going to be continual problems with perception and reality when it comes to issues of race in the game when the players are predominantly black and the fans are predominantly white. I think Martin Luther King Jr. addressed how any imbalance in life should be treated when he said, "Never look down on a man unless you're helping him to get up." Having been raised under the oppression of segregation in the South, I can tell you that the good doctor got it right.

Chapter 15

MOTIVATION AND WORK ETHIC

When I was young and choosing up sides on the playground, I purposely wouldn't pick the best kids. I didn't want to be on a team with the best players on it and win. I loved competition so much that I wanted to team up with the less renowned guys and find a way to win.

Whatever I got into, I was dedicated. My parents taught me to do my best in everything I did. Being the oldest of nine children, I was a role model before I even knew what the words meant. My parents always told me, "Walt, you've got to keep up the family name."

When my mom wasn't around, I was in charge. I had to walk my seven sisters and little brother to school. I learned patience because growing up with seven sisters, my mother, and my grandmother, I used to lie in bed each morning waiting for everyone to get ready. Growing up with women, I learned the importance of punctuality.

The buses, the ballparks, even the water fountains were segregated in the Atlanta I grew up in. There were places and neighborhoods I knew I shouldn't go to, but other guys would. I minded my own business. My parents and coaches used segregation to motivate and inspire me.

They'd say, "You've got to be twice as good as them."

I always pay homage to my parents, aunts, uncles, grandparents, teachers, and coaches. Even my peers in the playground helped me by not letting me smoke or drink or shoot craps. They said I was going to be an athlete and they weren't going to let me do anything negative that might hurt my chances of succeeding. I was truly raised by a village. My parents would tell me, "Son, you have to do this for the family." I was always cognizant of doing the right thing and projecting a positive image because I knew there were others following my progress and my example.

I never thought of becoming a pro basketball player. I never thought I had the talent. Even in my junior year at Southern Illinois when we played Louisville—the No. 2 team in the nation in 1966 with Wes Unseld and Butch Beard—and I averaged 25 points in the two games we played against them, I didn't think an NBA team would draft me. We had a big guy on our team named George McNeil and he got drafted in the eighth round, so when I did dream about it, I was like, "Man, I'd like to be drafted in the eighth round like George." Somehow starting out with nothing helped me get more than I ever dreamed.

My son was a pretty good basketball player. He played at the University of Pennsylvania and wanted to play professionally. But Walt III grew up in a very different environment than I did. When I used to visit him at his mother's home in Chicago, I would open the door to the refrigerator and it would be filled with all kinds of cans and bottles and food. As a kid, when I opened up the refrigerator in my house, the light in the back blinded me because there was hardly anything in it. After moving all the bottles and food out of the way, I used to point out to my son the light in the back of his refrigerator and say to him, "See that light, Walt? That light can be a beacon to your success." I don't know if my son would have made it to the NBA if he had my motivation. But he didn't. I'm just as proud of him and he went on to be a success in his own right, but he never fought his way to becoming a pro.

Players are not born great. They have to develop a tenacious work ethic before they can succeed. Bob Cousy was cut from his freshman and sophomore teams in high school. Michael Jordan was cut from his junior varsity high school basketball team. Now they start building young players up before they even start high school. These guys start believing their press clippings from a very early age. Guys who don't receive all that hoopla and who have less talent know they have to work harder. Bruce Bowen wouldn't be in the league today if he didn't become a defensive specialist. He played at Cal State Fullerton—not known as a basketball powerhouse—and in France and the Continental Basketball Association before he ever got his chance to play in the NBA. He developed savvy and the tenacious work ethic that usually only surfaces in a player who has overcome adversity in his career.

There are a lot of star players who display that hunger. Ginobili works hard. Kevin Garnett is the hardest-working guy in the game. He's always doubling up on defense, getting back to his man, running all over the court creating havoc. Jason Kidd, I get tired just watching him play. He steals the ball, dishes it out, comes back for the ball when his teammates are in trouble, he's up and down the court the entire game. Of course, Ben Wallace is another guy who makes up in effort what his game might be lacking in talent.

But there are too many guys in the league today who don't have the work ethic to improve their game. If a player is a poor free throw shooter, he stays a poor free throw shooter his entire career. If guys can't shoot the perimeter shot, they remain poor outside shooters their entire career. Whatever their weakness is, they can't seem to overcome it. The reason is that they lack the work ethic that has to be developed when players are young and hungry.

The NBA players today have no excuses. They don't need to have another job. All they have to do is work on that weakness, work on their game. They have to do that year-round, but they don't. They're out playing golf, they're traveling; they're doing other things. All the facilities are there for them. They have strict coaches. They have team doctors, trainers, and psychiatrists. Their workout gyms are beautiful.

Anyone playing in the NBA has to be dedicated. They have to love competition. They have to love to play. When I watch Marbury play, I can tell that the guy loves playing the game, although last year, his passion waned. The way I judge whether a guy loves to play or not is to ask him one simple question:

"Would you still be playing ball, even if you didn't get paid to do it?"

If a guy can answer me with a straight face, "Yes, no question," then I know he's telling me the truth. It's this love for the game, this drive to play and work hard, that separates good players from potential pro players.

In the summers when I played, we used to go to the Catskill Mountains in upstate New York to work at camps. Some of us used to visit three or four camps a day and run clinics. The kids wanted to see Willis and me play games of one-on-one so we would square off and Willis would kill me. He wanted to win so badly he squeezed the air out of the ball. I would have to let him get his shot because if I didn't Willis would've knocked me over.

It was a pickup game, but it was Willis's work ethic that made him play so hard. If you're going to do something, do it. Play 100 percent or don't play. I played those games of one-on-one with Willis because the kids wanted to see us play and I also got the chance to keep my defensive skills sharp. I didn't care if I won because I differentiated between playground games and organized ball—and I wasn't stupid enough to try to outmuscle Willis Reed. But I could appreciate Willis's work ethic. He became a star in the NBA coming out of a small black college in Louisiana—Grambling State University—and he tapped every ounce of skill and energy out of his body.

Reed played with a leg shot full of Novocain in Game 7 of the 1970 Finals. Bill Russell used to vomit before big games. Michael Jordan hugged the NBA championship trophy in the winning locker room like it was his long-lost brother. Magic Johnson came into the league without an outside shot and shooting a relatively low percentage on his free throws, but every summer he went back home and worked on those parts of his game. He became a deadly three-point shooter and after his third year in the league, he never shot below 80 percent from the charity stripe, leading the league one season shooting 91 percent.

Imagine how good today's players could be with that kind of dedication? What kind of havoc would Dirk Nowitzi cause if he became a real defensive stopper? Imagine the possibilities if Ben Wallace developed a 15-foot jumper. If Shaq ever became a good free throw shooter they'd just FedEx him the MVP Trophy every year. Now, all those guys work really hard. But to truly win the game within the game, they'll have to find the motivation to work harder every year.

I've always thought playing sports—but basketball in particular because of the continual momentum changes in the game—builds athletes' character. I've heard adages like the ones I'm going to present to you now many times before, but these have worked for me. Here they are. Take them for what they're worth.

CLYDE'S KEYS TO SUCCESS

1. Setting goals—Have a game plan.
2. Confidence—It sounds hackneyed, but if you
   don't believe in yourself, you can't achieve.
   Don't leave home without your confidence.

3. Utilization of time—We're all given 24 hours in a day so it's up to us to maximize our time. Don't procrastinate, devastate.

4. Motivation—It comes from the inside out, not the outside in.

5. Work ethic—Be tenacious, hell-bent, possessed for what you want. Be willing to work for it.

6. Communication—You can't motivate unless you communicate.

7. Teamwork—Working together, sharing, and caring.

8. Luck—Sometimes it's better to be lucky than good.

9. Worship—Even if it's a rock, believe in something.

I nearly lost my life when I was living in my house in St. Croix in the U.S. Virgin Islands when Hurricane Hugo hit the island in 1989. The eye of the hurricane struck the island dead center and I had to go into my bathroom—the only secure room in the house—and wait out the storm for 14 hours until it stopped. With winds of more than 155 miles per hour, Hugo was life-threatening; playing basketball is not. But you learn from playing the game that when things look hopeless, you can't bail out. You have to hang in and struggle to go on.

A lot of people told me that I should leave St. Croix after Hugo had destroyed my house and much of my property. But I just stuck it out and rebuilt my house. In basketball, you learn how to overcome difficult situations and to always be optimistic that things are going to get better. I couldn't run away.

I guess that's why I never did drugs. Drugs are just a way of forgetting about today. But when you come down from your drug trip, the problem is still there. So you can only prolong it. In basketball, as in life, you have to deal with your problems—not put them off—and rise to the challenges.

I never looked at playing basketball as being a job like so many of my peers did. They let themselves go after their playing careers because training, for them, was only done so that they could keep their livelihood. But training and working out is my lifestyle. They played and kept in shape because it was their job. That's why when I see so many former NBA players from my era today, they're out of shape. I went running in Central Park this morning. People are always telling me I look in great shape. Vanity, vanity, all is vanity. But my work ethic and attention to fitness to this day also have a lot to do with the tenacity I developed as a kid playing basketball every day. The game influenced and shaped my life in so many ways.

Chapter 16

THE GREATEST TEAMS AND
HALL OF FAME PLAYERS

Over the years there have been players who have shown the will to win the game within the game. And occasionally this mastery has been shared by an entire team. The best team I ever saw was the 1966–67 Philadelphia 76ers. That team had talent. My body aches just thinking about them. Besides Wilt at center, they had Luke Jackson, Chet Walker, Wali Jones, and Hal Greer rounding out the starting five, with Billy Cunningham coming off the bench. They were able to beat the Celtics in five games in the Eastern Division finals because Wilt wasn't concerned with scoring. He had averaged 39.5 points per game in his first seven seasons in the league, but that season Wilt averaged only 24 points per game, while also averaging nearly 8 assists and 24 rebounds per game. The Sixers won 68 games during the regular season and beat the San Francisco Warriors led by Rick Barry and Nate Thurmond, in six games in the NBA Finals.

Growing up, I hated the Celtics because they won all

the time. I admired and respected them because they were such great champions, but I never liked them. I liked Wilt, not Russell. Wilt was cool. He had the goatee and he used to hang out. So I always rooted for Wilt, Hal Greer, and the Sixers, and they always lost to the Celtics, except for 1967.

The only teams to beat the Celtics in that 13-year span were the St. Louis Hawks in 1958—a team that included Bob Pettit, Cliff Hagan, and Clyde Lovellette, who in 1959 became the first three players on an NBA team ever to average more than 20 points a game each for an entire season—and the Sixers in 1967.

Russell was the guy. The Sixers always had the better team—they won more games in the regular season—but they only beat the Celtics that one year. Under pressure, the Sixers always threw the ball away or did something else wrong to lose the big games. The Celtics always rose to the occasion. With Russell guarding the basket, they could stop teams when they needed a stop to win a game.

I've heard a lot of people say that Wilt was more concerned with his personal scoring and rebounding numbers than with winning championships, but I disagree. Wilt had the numbers and a winning attitude; in the big games his teams often came close, but mostly they failed to win because of one man.

Following the 1967–68 season, the Sixers traded Wilt to the Lakers for Darrall Imhoff and Archie Clark and the Sixers didn't win another NBA championship for 15 years, when Dr. J and Moses Malone and company swept the Lakers in four games in 1983. Wilt was making $100,000 a year, and that was a lot of money in those days when teams were just barely prospering. The only player making more was Bill Russell. The Celtics paid him $100,001.

The Celtics were just too good in those days. The Phoenix Suns could learn a lot about winning championships by watching old game tapes of the Russell-led Celtics teams. They ran, but they also played defense. For the Russell teams, defense was their best offense. The Celtics funneled their opponents into the lane toward Russell and he started their fast break off by blocking shots. No other player in the game has ever started his team's transition game the way Russell did. Ben Wallace plays a little like Russell did, but Russell kept you honest if you dropped off him. He could shoot a little jumper and he had a nice hook shot.

The Russell-Chamberlain matchup was the greatest in NBA history and probably the greatest ever in all of professional sports. In the span of six years (1964 to 1969), Wilt and Russell went head-to-head in 87 games, the equivalent of more than a full NBA season. Where other teams would routinely have Wilt triple- and even quadruple-teamed, the Celtics pretty much had Russell guard Chamberlain one-on-one, with Satch Sanders helping out from time to time.

The NBA when I was growing up was watching Wilt play Russell every Sunday in the Game of the Week and then seeing the Celtics play the Lakers with West and Baylor in the Finals. Oscar Robertson was the only other player in the league who was renowned and received media attention. I hardly knew anything about the rest of the teams.

The Minneapolis Lakers and George Mikan were the

first dominant team and player in the NBA, winning five out of six championships between 1949 and 1954. In 1950, when the Lakers won their second NBA championship, the league had expanded from its original 11 teams in 1946 to 17 teams. The Rochester Royals in 1951 were the only team to beat the Lakers in that six-year span. The Royals' point guard was one William "Red" Holzman.

Mikan was so provocative a player because he was the first overpowering big man in the game at six foot ten. In those days, the top big men besides Mikan were Dolph Schayes, Vern Mikkelsen, Neil Johnston, and "Easy Ed" Macauley, and they were all six foot eight. The Knicks' biggest men were Connie Simmons at six foot eight and Harry "the Horse" Gallatin at six foot six.

If Russell and Chamberlain were the NBA in the 1960s, George Mikan was the NBA all by himself in the 1950s. There is a famous photo of Mikan standing on a ladder, polishing with a white hanky the bold black letters of his name written on the marquee outside Madison Square Garden that read, "Geo Mikan vs. Knicks."

The Celtics dynasty of the late '50s and '60s will never happen again because in today's NBA, it's impossible to keep a team together that long. Russell played with Bob Cousy for seven years and with John Havlicek for seven years, winning six championships with each accompanying star. The combination of free agency, the money players make today, and the salary cap makes keeping a dominant team like that together for 13 years running a thing of the past. The closest any team has gotten since to the Celtics dynasty was the Lakers' run of five championships in nine years in the 1980s and the Bulls' string of six championships in eight years in the 1990s.

Dynasties are good for basketball. It's always good to have a team that everybody hates. It generates a lot of interest. Our Knick championship teams were rare in that we didn't have one player that the other teams' fans loved to hate. We were revered like the great Celtics teams of the '80s. But every team that wins multiple championships in a short span of time usually attracts its fair share of scorn from opposing teams' fans.

The greatest teams that won over a span of at least four years were the Celtics of the 1960s, the Knicks of the early 1970s, the Celtics and Lakers of the 1980s, the Bulls of the early 1990s, and the Lakers of the late 1990s. I never saw Mikan's Lakers so I can't comment on their dominance in that era.

The greatest single-season team ever was the 1966–67 76er team, followed by the 1970–71 Milwaukee Bucks, with Abdul-Jabbar averaging nearly 35 points per game, plus Oscar Robertson and Bobby Dandridge. Two other great one-season-wonder teams were the 1971–72 Lakers, still with Wilt, West, and Goodrich, and the 1982–83 Philadelphia 76ers, led by Dr. J, Moses Malone, Maurice Cheeks, and Andrew Toney. The Sixers won 65 games in the regular season and went 12-1 in the playoffs, sweeping the defending champion Lakers in the Finals.

One could make a claim for the Lakers of 2000 to 2004 as being the greatest team of all time. They won three straight championships and lost in the 2004 Finals to the Pistons. Certainly Shaq and Kobe were a dynamic one-two punch and Phil is a great coach, but look at their Finals' competition: They beat the Indiana Pacers in their only NBA Finals appearance, the Sixers in their first Finals appearance since 1983, and the Nets in their first-ever NBA Finals appearance.

The "Bad Boys" Pistons of 1987 to 1990, who won two championships, and lost in seven games to the Lakers in the 1988 Finals and in seven games to the Celtics in the 1987 Eastern Conference finals, can certainly make a claim too. But by the time they came along, the two great teams of the '80s, the Celtics and the Lakers, were aging, and the Pistons' successor, the Bulls, were just coming together. They had a great backcourt in Isiah, Dumars, and Vinnie Johnson, but their frontcourt will be remembered more for their physical play than their greatness.

Even the Celtics of the 1970s with Havlicek, Cowens, JoJo White, and Paul Silas, who won two championships in three years ('74 and '76) and lost to the Knicks in seven games in the 1973 Eastern Conference finals, can lay claim to being one of the greatest. Havlicek won eight championships with three different coaches and three different casts of Celtics players and, at age 38 in his final NBA season, he played in all 82 regular-season games and averaged 16 points per contest. But I don't consider those Celtics teams as amongst the best five ever because, while Havlicek was great, and Cowens is in the Hall of Fame, the rest of their players were not exceptional.

The Spurs were dethroned by the Mavericks last season, but they still might be on the verge of a dynasty with their young nucleus of Duncan, who is 30, Parker, 24, and Ginobili, 29. They have already won three championships (1999, 2003, and 2005). Time will tell whether they can become a team of the ages or whether the Suns, Mavs, the Pistons, or the Heat will step up and foil their chance to be a team of history. And, if Shaq and D. Wade stay together, the Heat could make a run at greatness too.

It is in the playoffs that great teams and great players distinguish themselves. To win in the playoffs is the ultimate. No matter what you do in the regular season, nobody's going to care if you don't win in the playoffs. As a player, my two best statistical seasons were in 1971 and 1972. I was first team All-Pro, All-Defensive First Team, and an All-Star both years, but it meant nothing because the Knicks lost in the playoffs both years.

The 1995–96 Bulls, the team with the greatest overall record in NBA history, won 72 games in the regular season and went 15-3 over four playoff series, but when the Seattle SuperSonics came back from 3-0 in the Finals to win two straight games, the Bulls were worried. Ron Harper had T-shirts made up saying, "72 Wins Don't Mean a Thing, Without the Ring."

If you look at many of the great players: Pettit, Greer, West, Russell, Reed, Havlicek, Rick Barry, Cowens, Dr. J, Abdul-Jabbar, Magic, Bird, and Jordan, they all averaged more points per game in their peak seasons in the playoffs than they did during their best regular seasons.

When you look at the great player-matchups in Finals history, certainly Chamberlain and Russell, who faced each other in two Finals, 1964 and 1969, dwarf all the others. They were two Goliaths going at it. Chamberlain always had the massive advantage statistically—averaging 29 points per game to Russell's 11 points per game in the

'64 Finals—but Russell and the Celtics prevailed over Wilt's Warriors and Lakers.

Although Jerry West and I did not guard each other most of the time, our duel in the 1970 Finals was probably the greatest backcourt encounter in NBA Finals history. When I switched off and did defend West, I tried to force him to his left and keep him in front of me. I knew he liked to start quickly and stop suddenly to shoot the jumper. When he guarded me, he'd let me penetrate—knowing I had to look out for Chamberlain—and then he'd try to reach around me and knock the ball loose or block my shot from behind. He always made me think, and just doing that made me predictable because I was thinking rather than reacting.

West made the greatest shot in Finals history in Game 3 of that series, swishing a 60-foot shot at the buzzer to tie the game in regulation. I remember the determination on his face. He was hell-bent to make that shot. Chamberlain was already in the locker room. They had to go get him out for the overtime. Nobody thought West could make that shot. If there had been a three-point shot back then, it would've won the game for the Lakers and there may never have been a Game 7.

The most prolific scoring spree between two rival players in the history of the Finals occurred when Michael Jordan and Charles Barkley matched their prodigious scoring appetites. Jordan scored 246 points to Sir Charles's 164 points over six games. Jordan's average of 41 points per game set a Finals record, but Barkley's 27 points a contest wasn't paltry either.

The greatest dunk in NBA Finals history was either

Dr. J's windmill dunk over Michael Cooper in 1983 or his "Statue of Liberty" dunk over Bill Walton in Game 1 of the 1977 Finals. Afterward, Dr. J said about hammering home the dunk against Walton, "I'll challenge anybody." The Doc had those huge hands and that amazing leaping ability that put any dunk he could imagine within his reach.

Although Hakeem Olajuwon and Patrick Ewing didn't always go head-to-head in the '94 Finals, their matchup was probably the most riveting between two seven-footers in NBA Finals history. Olajuwon totally outplayed Shaq in the '95 Finals, but Ewing held his own against the Dream, averaging 19 points per game to Olajuwon's 27 points per game, and outrebounding Hakeem and blocking more shots during the series. But Ewing shot only 36 percent from the field while Olajuwon hit on 50 percent of his shots.

Bird and Magic faced each other in 3 Finals in the 1980s and their rivalry—like Ewing and Olajuwon's—was a continuation of their great NCAA championship game encounter. Neither Magic nor Bird played devastating, man-to-man defense. They played good team defense, but they were mostly offensive players that played with great savvy and instinctual prowess. They both had a tremendous will to win that lifted their teammates to play as if each possession were a battle.

The Jordan-Barkley showdown in the 1993 Finals between the Bulls and the Suns was not only a clash of two flamboyant stars, but two teams with very different collective personalities. The Bulls were a great defensive team who ran the triangle offense with precision. The

Suns were a lot like the Suns of 2004—a high-flying bunch, led by Barkley and Kevin Johnson.

I loved the way KJ played. He was an old-school guard. He could do it all: shoot off the dribble, run the pick-and-roll, and handle the playmaking duties. He was fearless, a fantastic player. But Jordan and Pippen were in their prime. They played one of the greatest games in the history of the Finals in Game 3 in Chicago when the Suns beat the Bulls 129–121 in triple overtime, reminding fans of probably *the* greatest single game in NBA Finals history, when the Suns lost a triple-overtime game to the Celtics in Boston Garden, 128–126, back in 1976.

The Bulls-Jazz Finals in 1998 was equally dramatic. Just as when Barkley was named the MVP of the league in 1993, Jordan had something to prove once more when Karl Malone was named the MVP of the league in 1998. The Bulls, particularly Rodman, who guarded Malone, took Karl out of his element. They were doubling and tripling him and they forced Karl to shoot fallaway jumpers. The way Michael won the final game—stealing the ball and then hitting a 20-foot jumper with under 10 seconds left in the game—was so vivid and exciting.

The great teams and players love to play with their back against the wall. Nobody thought Chamberlain could give up his prodigious scoring to become a team player and win a championship, but he did in 1967, and again in 1972.

Few thought that Russell, at the age of 37—when Boston finished in fourth place in the Eastern Division during the regular season with only 48 wins—would be able to beat the Lakers in the 1969 Finals. Russell was in his last year. He had had leg injuries during the season that forced him to be hospitalized.

And few thought that after coming out of retirement in 1995 and getting beaten by the Orlando Magic in the playoffs, Michael Jordan and his Bulls would return to win championships. But they defied popular belief by winning three straight titles (1996 to 1998).

Jordan—like Russell in 1969—walked off into the sunset, retiring as a champion, when his crossover dribble against Jazz defender Byron Russell and game-winning shot made the Bulls six-time champions. But temptation got the better of Michael. He returned from his second retirement in 2001 and tried to take the lowly Washington Wizards to the Promised Land. But Michael finally met a challenge on the basketball court that he could not defeat. In two seasons with Washington, Michael the Wizard didn't make it back to the playoffs in the East.

The greatest teams and Hall of Fame players always perform better on the road where they know how to come out and play well from the get-go. No one wants to play catch-up on the road. You have to keep the other team's crowd out of it. At home, you can play from behind because you have the adrenaline of the crowd on your side, but on the road, in hostile environments—where you only have your teammates to rely on—is where the great teams and players excel. They know how to block out the crowd and their greatness is actually piqued when opposing fans think they can intimidate them.

The great teams run away with games, beating their opponents by big margins. The Celtics did it in the '50s and '60s. When the Knicks were rampaging in the '70s, I remember that by the third quarter we would be beating teams by 17 or 18 points. The 1971–72 Lakers ran away with games. The lesser teams in the league can't compete. Only the elite teams can keep up, and the great teams still beat them by eight or nine points.

I tell kids at my summer basketball camp that if they want to become great players, they cannot have any weaknesses. "If you can't go to your left," I say, "you have a weakness and I'm going to force you to it." When I guarded Robertson, West, the Pearl, or Hondo, they always found a way to improvise and create havoc. It was difficult to take them out of their game because they could do so many things that a defender couldn't stop.

"Hall of Famers," I tell kids, "have no weaknesses."

Great players overcome defenses and rules that have been set up to stop them. Mikan still won three championships after the NBA expanded the foul lane to prevent him from setting up too close to the basket and Chamberlain won his two championships after the lane was further expanded to try and stop him.

After UCLA went undefeated in Kareem Abdul-Jabbar's sophomore season (1966–67), the NCAA instituted a no-dunking rule, a backhanded compliment to Kareem. As a result, the skyhook was born. Otherwise, Kareem would have been like Shaq, a tall guy overwhelming people. Challenged with having to develop a shot to overcome the no-dunking rule, Kareem developed the most lethal shot in the history of the game.

Great players don't have to be flashy. Oscar was the most fundamentally sound player I've ever seen. He was so big he could overwhelm you. He understood the game, was a master of the pick-and-roll, was an excellent passer and rebounder, and he always got his shot up. He was a team player and a pressure player, a serious competitor. In his prime, he averaged 30 points, 11 assists, and close to 10 rebounds a game.

My five greatest players of all time would be: Bill Russell—who has more championship rings than fingers; Oscar Robertson—the Big O, the game's most versatile player and my idol early on; Kareem Abdul-Jabbar—the most unheralded of the big men; Dr. J—the most provocative player the game has ever seen; and Michael Jordan—who dominated the game with his acrobatics and will.

Of the players today, Duncan is the best overall. Kevin Garnett is the most talented. Shaq is the most dominating— with his gargantuan size, there is no one in the game today who can defend him. Chamberlain always had Russell, but Shaq has no one to deny him. He has no rival. He's invincible.

Jason Kidd is still the best point guard in the league. I like Kobe because he plays D. McGrady has the potential to be great, but he still likes to score too much. Nowitzki is a great shooter and he can post up defenders, making him a formidable matchup. Dwyane Wade is a real force in this league who has proven that he can dominate a game through sheer will. Ginobili is a great team player who just seems to keep getting better. His challenge in the years to come will be whether he will remain a great team player now that he has reached personal stardom.

LeBron still has a few more years of being humble left. Although he really showed me something during last season's playoff run. He's like Michael was early on in his career when the Bulls couldn't get by the Pistons. LeBron will have to stay humble until he gets a better team around him. Then he'll change. LeBron will change. Right now he's expending too much energy, trying to play the roles of playmaker, finisher, and savior. LeBron has to learn how to conserve energy. The star player always has to save a little extra energy for the clutch when he knows the ball is coming to him. He can't be tired. If LeBron learns how to post up his man rather than play out on the perimeter and drive to the basket, he could rest and save his energy and greatness for down the stretch of big games—when it really matters.

Muhammad Ali was famous for his Ali shuffle early in his career, but then he learned he could be equally successful employing the Rope-A-Dope. Jordan began his NBA career as a high-flyer who tried to win games all by himself, but he adjusted with age and wisdom to scoring more consistently with his back to the basket and setting up his teammates. Greatness is the ability to change your game and still be as successful—perhaps even more successful—than you were in your previous incarnation.

The great players are relentless. Hal Greer made me foul out in my first preseason game—and cry afterward—because I couldn't do anything with the guy. He just killed me. He kept on running the pick-and-roll and hitting 15-foot jumpers. And this was the preseason, and I was a rookie he had probably never heard of at that moment in time. As Satchel Paige said, "Don't look back, they might be gaining on you."

Bill Russell's competitiveness still knows no bounds.

At 72, he still doesn't sign autographs, even for former players. Willis asked him for his autograph last year during the Legends Tour and Russell declined. Willis was flabbergasted. But Russell is just a stubborn, hard guy. He wouldn't sign for Willis. Russell doesn't sign for any former player and it probably stems from his playing days when, except for Wilt, he didn't show any friendliness to opposing players.

Great teams need an identity, timing, and luck. The coaches and star players have the responsibility to establish that team identity and then the great teams create their own luck. Timing is part of that luck, but then the rest has to be left to the gods. Winning championships can't be taken for granted. The 2004 Lakers with four future Hall of Fame players in their starting five were preordained to win one, but the Pistons got in the way.

To be a great team, you have to beat your top rivals. That is the beauty of basketball. There are great team rivalries and astounding player duels. A great team doesn't achieve a for-the-ages status until it conquers its toughest rivals at least twice in the playoffs. A great player doesn't get inducted into the Hall of Fame without dominating the other great players he faces in key playoff matchups. The road to greatness of the game within the game is marked with challenges and triumphs.

Chapter 17

Conclusion:
Winning the Game Within the Game

I've got to be honest with you; if I were playing today I think I'd average pretty close to a triple double every night. Say around 21 points, 9 assists, and 8 rebounds per game. I'm not trying to brag or anything, I'm just being realistic. I averaged 19 points a game back when the defender was allowed to put his hands on you. You've got to give me a few more now. My assists would go up because when I played you only got an assist if a pass led directly to a bucket. And with all the long rebounds coming from three point shots these days, I'd definitely grab a few more rebounds. Even though today's players are physically unlike anything I had to deal with back in the day, I know I could compete with any of them. That's because I worked hard to win the game within the game.

I mastered the team game and played with other highly skilled players who accentuated my strengths and helped hide my weaknesses. I watched them for long enough and learned so much from them that, after a while, I didn't really have any weaknesses. Can you imagine what today's superstars would be like if they didn't have any weaknesses? Who could deal with Dirk Nowitzki if he became a lockdown defender? Shaq would be unbeatable if he shot 90% from the free throw line. And nobody would be able to stop LeBron James if he shot lights out from three point range and developed a strong post-up game.

Kobe Bryant is already a prolific scorer and a great defender. But imagine the possibilities if he truly mastered the team game. As great as Steve Nash is, opposing guards still feel they can score against him.

Winning the game within the game is about making your teammates better. It's about accentuating team play. It's about fine-tuning your timing. It's about approaching the game from a psychological and intuitive standpoint as well as a physical one. It's about making sacrifices and, at times, muting your individual game to increase the team's balance and flow. The step-back three pointer and the tomahawk dunk have their place in the game within the game, but only if those shots don't detract from the fluidity and rhythm of the team game. It's about vision and movement, keeping your head up and seeing the floor so you can make good passes or catch bad ones. It's about never standing still unless you're setting a pick.

I'm excited about basketball. I haven't played professionally in thirty years but the sound of sneakers squeaking against a gym floor still gets my juices flowing. The NBA is the best of the best in the basketball universe and it has been an honor and a privilege for me to make my living in that world. The things I see on a nightly basis during the season amaze and delight me. These guys are good. For real.

But there's always room for improvement and everyone can learn from the past. The game of basketball should be passed down from generation to generation, from player to player. For whatever it's worth, this book is a collection of what I have to offer. This is what I can pass down to today's players and to the youngsters coming up after them. I truly believe that, if players of all skill levels dedicate themselves to studying and winning the game within the game, there's no limit to the astounding heights that the game of basketball can reach.

Jump ball, people. Who wants it?